WINNING
THE BRAIN
RACE

A publication of the
Center for Self-Governance

WINNING THE BRAIN RACE

A Bold Plan to Make Our Schools Competitive

Revised and Updated

David T. Kearns and Denis P. Doyle

ICS Press

San Francisco, California

© 1991 David T. Kearns and Denis P. Doyle

This book is a publication of the Center for Self-Governance, dedicated to the study of self-governing institutions. The Center is affiliated with the Institute for Contemporary Studies, a nonpartisan, nonprofit public policy research organization. The analyses, conclusions, and opinions expressed in ICS Press publications are those of the authors and not necessarily those of the Institute or its officers, directors, or others associated with, or funding, its work.

Inquiries, book orders, and catalog requests should be addressed to ICS Press, Institute for Contemporary Studies, 720 Market Street, San Francisco, CA 94102. (415) 981-5353. FAX: (415) 986-4878. To order, call toll free (800) 326-0263 in the United States.

0 9 8 7 6 5 4 3

Library of Congress Cataloging-in-Publication Data

Kearns, David T.
    Winning the brain race : a bold plan to make our schools competitive / David T. Kearns and Denis P. Doyle. – Rev. and updated.
        p.   cm.
    ISBN 1-55815-166-4 : $10.95
    1. Education–United States–Aims and objectives.   2. Public schools–United States–Evaluation.   3. Industry and education–United States.   I. Doyle, Denis P.   II. Title.
LA217.K43   1991
370'.973–dc20   91-3907
                                                                             CIP

To my family, particularly my own children, who taught me the value of education

DTK

To my father—who taught me to write; to my mother—who taught me to care; to my wife—who taught me about courage

DPD

Human history becomes more and more a race between education and catastrophe.

—H. G. Wells

CONTENTS

FOREWORD

Since its publication in 1988, *Winning the Brain Race* has changed the way people think about schools. David Kearns and Denis Doyle's six-point plan for restructuring our education system has influenced everyone who cares about education, from individual teachers to the nation's highest officials. This updated edition tells us what we have accomplished—and what is left to be done.

David Kearns, a businessman, and Denis Doyle, an academic, have proposed public education reforms that apply the concepts of the marketplace to our schools. To create schools that are self-governing, productive enterprises, their plan supports six goals: (1) choice for parents, students, and teachers; (2) school restructuring from the bottom up; (3) professionalism in teaching; (4) academic standards; (5) a core curriculum that teaches the values of democracy and citizenship; and (6) an increased federal role in research.

Choice—the idea that students should be able to choose the schools where they learn—was a novel, and not very popular, idea when the authors first presented it. Today, school districts across the country have implemented magnet school programs, and surveys show that over half the population supports school choice in some form.

Why are we so concerned about the future of our schools? Why do we need to "win" the brain race? Because a strong society and a healthy U.S. economy depend on the ability of American enterprises to compete successfully with foreign companies. And successful American enterprises rely primarily on the skills of an educated workforce. Unfortunately, U.S. companies currently must spend millions of dollars every year providing remedial training for their employees—a burden our competitors do not share. To remain competitive, our schools must provide better and more effective education, from day care through high school.

In one sense implementing the authors' plan will be difficult, because the changes need to be so comprehensive. In another sense, it will be simple, because we don't need to wait for the federal government to act: you and I, our neighborhoods and our communities, can do it—school by school, district by district. Who knows better what our schools need than those who actually use them? And Kearns and Doyle provide both the plan and the strategy—they tell us *how* schools should reorganize, *who* should be in charge, and *where* the money should come from.

Winning the Brain Race targets the year 2000 for implementing all aspects of these bold reforms. If the education community fails to respond, public schools will likely continue to decline and private schools will become increasingly attractive—to those who can afford them. We believe these reforms will help our public schools become self-governing and produce the educated workforce we need to keep America competitive.

Robert B. Hawkins, Jr.
President
Institute for Contemporary Studies

ACKNOWLEDGMENTS

This book draws on our very different experiences in the worlds of business and public education. Those two worlds rarely meet, and we hope that our differences combine to produce more than the sum of the parts. That at least was our intention. We think each has much to learn from the other.

In the same spirit, we wish to acknowledge our intellectual debts. Our most abiding debt is to the public schools of which we are both products. They were not perfect institutions, but they nurtured us and held us to high standards. We hope to return the favor.

In addition to our institutional debt, we owe special thanks to former teachers, family, friends, colleagues, and critics. They have shaped our thinking about the important issues we raise in this book. To all those to whom we are in debt, but unable to acknowledge by name, we nevertheless extend our heartfelt thanks.

This new edition of *Winning the Brain Race* differs in three important ways from the original. It has been updated, noting, where appropriate, new developments since its original release; the original Chapter 1 and Chapter 8 have been combined to create a new Chapter 8; and a new Chapter 1 has been added, written in its entirety by Denis P. Doyle. In light of his appointment as U.S. deputy secretary of education in May 1991, David T. Kearns did not participate in the preparation of the new Chapter 1.

There are, however, two people without whom this book would have been impossible, Vic Pesqueira and Renate Banks of Xerox. Their knowledge, good humor, patience, and editorial assistance helped bring this book to completion in record time.

We would also like to acknowledge Julie Ellis of ICS and Carolyn McGovern for their invaluable editorial assistance.

We must, of course, accept full responsibility for any errors of fact.

David T. Kearns
Denis P. Doyle

WINNING
THE BRAIN
RACE

1

The Challenge and the Opportunity

Denis P. Doyle

The federal government can show leadership, but the only way we're going to improve our schools—and therefore our country—is one student at a time, one school at a time, one school system at a time.
—John F. Akers
CEO, IBM
Chairman, Business Roundtable Education Task Force

BY TEMPERAMENT AND TRADITION Americans are optimists. We believe that our life chances and the life chances of our children can be improved by hard work, diligence, and enterprise. We know that we are a favored people—our political and economic traditions are models for the world; our climate is benign and our natural resources vast. We enjoy the benefits of a continental common market; our neighbors are friends; we have not been invaded since the British burned the White House in 1812. We enjoy extraordinary agricultural and material abundance. People move freely both to and from and within our country.

Our institutions are democratic, our markets are free, our habits are egalitarian. Could Americans be anything other than optimists? Ordinarily this quality is a great asset. No longer. Today optimism—at least about education—is a fool's paradise.

This optimism leads to a disconcerting and potentially dangerous development—the conviction of most Americans that education is in deep trouble but that the problem is someone else's schools. As long as we continue to believe this, the problem will get worse, not better.

The first edition of *Winning the Brain Race: A Bold Plan to Make Our Schools Competitive* was written in the fall and winter of 1987–1988 and released May 17, 1988. David Kearns and I presented the first copy to then–vice-president George Bush in his office in the Old Executive Office Building. With us at that meeting was University of Tennessee president Lamar Alexander. Since that bright spring morning, much has changed, yet much has remained the same.

We were convinced then—as we are now—that the nation faces an education crisis. And most Americans agree. Yet too little has been done. Why? There is a profound irony in the "education crisis": Almost without exception, Americans believe that it is someone else's problem. The reasons, which are not hard to fathom, bear brief examination. And they are the reasons for this new edition.

The education crisis raises the most troubling problem a democracy can face: When opinion leaders—"natural aristocrats," to borrow Thomas Jefferson's term—do not lead, change does not occur. The poor and dispossessed, arguably those most in need of education reform, are least able to pursue it. And those best able to pursue it—men and women who by position, knowledge, and ability could make a difference—do not because they don't see the problem's severity.

This lack of perception is aptly characterized as the "frog's dilemma": Drop a frog into boiling water and out it leaps. Plunge a frog into tepid water and turn up the heat slowly—it will be overcome by languor, unable to extricate itself until it is too late.

That is where America stands today—aware that there is a

problem, yet not convinced the problem is "ours." Indeed, in many cases, we are convinced the problem is someone else's and does not merit our attention or effort.

If we could do only one thing to improve our schools it would be disabuse all Americans of the notion that "it is someone else's problem." It is our problem, and recognizing that is the first of many steps needed to improve our schools.

A narrow view of "the problem," of course, is not unique to education. It permeates thinking in other institutions as well. American business, for example, let its guard down in the 1970s. Coasting on a reputation earned during and after World War II, American manufacturers thought they could do no wrong. Particularly in business and commerce, the race goes to the swift, and the penalty for losing has been harsh and painful. We have lost not only market share but whole industries to foreign competitors. America invented and used to "own" electronics, televisions, high-performance automobiles, facsimile transmission, the computer chip, PCs—the list is long and dreary.

As every American knows, we must now scramble to keep up; and in a competitive world economy "keeping up" is not enough. If we are to prosper in the next century, we must "leapfrog" ahead, outdistancing the competition (which itself is constantly moving forward) to position ourselves for the next generation of competitive pressures. Being "as good" will not be good enough, not in business and not in education. We must set our sights on being better.

But the news is not all bad. Recent evidence indicates that the American industrial might that was once the envy of the world is making a strong comeback. Corporations as diverse as Cummins Engine, General Electric, Caterpillar Tractor, and Xerox are not only rebounding, they are regaining market share. They have done so because they have learned hard lessons at great pain. But the lessons have been learned well.

Are there lessons in this for the schools? There are two: We can recover and reclaim the legacy, and we must face our problems squarely. "Know the truth and the truth will set you free" is an old adage. And it is the necessary first step if we are to succeed.

The first task of the education reformer, then, is to raise the alarm. Play Paul Revere.

The second task is to propose remedies to the problems before us. We undertook both assignments in the first edition of this book. We attempted to sound the alarm—without being alarmist—and advanced a set of remedies that we were convinced would work. In hindsight, I am more convinced than ever that they can work.

The third task is implementation. Put ideas in place. Make them work. In the parlance of business, after the R & D and marketing studies, prepare for "rollout." And the ideas we advanced in the first edition of *Winning the Brain Race* are more than ready for rollout. If evidence is needed, the experience of the past three years offers it. The ideas were originally spelled out in detail in six chapters; they follow, updated and refined, in Chapters 2 through 7.

I am pleased that our ideas have withstood the test of time. There is a reason, to be sure: As we observed in the first edition, the power of our ideas is not their novelty or originality, but precisely the fact that they are tested, tried and true. The original aspect of *Winning the Brain Race*, then, is not what we proposed, but that what we proposed is in one place. We knit together a seamless web of reform, not piecemeal, but as a package within reach of any school in America. Why did we use this approach? Because it produces "synergy," a process in which the total result is more than the sum of the parts. An old idea in the world of high technology and science, synergy is the secret. Ideas do not stand alone. In combining ideas energy is released. This simple fact explains why it is often so difficult for new ideas to be adopted. At some atavistic level, in some dim memory of times past, we may remember just how demanding transitions are.

Change is difficult. Any significant innovation unleashes a chain of consequences that are almost impossible to foresee. A new technology, for example, precipitates a host of changes in social and organizational relationships. The introduction of the tractor not only replaces the horse, it changes a chain of relationships, both upstream and downstream, from harness makers and horseshoers, to oil drillers and machinists. And it transforms horizontal relationships as well, within both the farmer's family and the farmer's community. New technologies are more than mechanical devices; they rearrange the social and the cultural landscape.

Even when we recognize this, however, the pace of change is disappointingly slow. Indeed, in education our worst fears have materialized. Neither the public nor educators have forced the pace of reform and restructuring. In fact, both have avoided the painful task.

But this too has a reason, one that should not be surprising. Three years ago we described the schools as a "failed public monopoly" and were accused of using strong, even intemperate language. But the events of the past three years convince me that the charge was on target.

We argued then that the reason business restructured—and schools had not—was that business was driven by dire necessity. Restructure or die. Monopolies, however, die slowly. Not driven by dire necessity, they hang on, and on—until they too are forced by circumstance to change. What makes monopolies change? Even they are eventually subject to market forces—unless government arbitrarily and inappropriately protects them with statute.

Tariffs are one example of such protection, licenses are another. Tariffs and licenses, singly or together, create exclusive or semi-exclusive franchises, time-tested devices to protect the inefficient producer. Usually defended on specious public interest grounds, their effort is to limit trade and penalize the consumer. At their most extreme, they are found in totalitarian states, where monopolies are the norm. Called "private" monopolies in right-wing regimes, they differ only in name from the state monopolies of left-wing regimes. Both are creatures of the state, given authority and power by design. The losers are workers and consumers, the winners plutocrats and *apparatchiks*.

But monopolies have no place in a free society, unless no other form of organization will serve the public interest. Accordingly, we give monopoly power to the police and the military, preferring state action to private action in these spheres. But there is little else in the modern, high-tech world that deserves

monopoly protection. We once protected the postal service—
until delivery became so slow and problematic that an enterpris-
ing alternative was developed. Federal Express filled a niche that
the U.S. Postal Service could have—at least in theory. Why did
the post office fail to offer overnight delivery service? Because it
was protected. And now that it is not protected, Federal Express,
DHL, Airborne, and other overnight shippers have appeared.
The post office has lost customers it may never regain, and
"new" customers have been created, users who never knew they
"needed" overnight delivery until it was available!

So too the monopoly of Ma Bell has ended, and though the
transition to competition in the phone industry has been rocky
for some, on balance the market has served all our interests with
greater efficiency than the old monopoly.

We were, of course, aware of these trends when we wrote
the first edition, but we were reluctant then to expose the public
schools to the pressure of direct private sector competition. We
originally argued that the public schools needed time to get their
house in order; we supported a level playing field that would
treat public and private providers equally. Indeed, our fear was
that with untrammeled competition, the public schools would
languish, perhaps fade away altogether. As perhaps they might.
But they no longer need or deserve monopoly protection. To the
contrary, it is time to end the monopoly, end the exclusive franchise.

The public schools have enormous resources—intellectual,
administrative, and financial—and they can be expected to meet
the challenge that private schools offer. If they do not, they have
no one to blame but themselves. It is by now clear that that
challenge will take several forms. First, conventional, not-for-
profit private schools are continuing to increase their share of
enrollment. While the largest providers of private education in
the nation—the Catholic schools—are shrinking, their enrollment decline is caused by a number of complex factors having to
do with demographic and ecclesiastical changes that are beyond
the scope of this short book. The rest of the private school market
continues to grow.

Second, a small but growing number of for-profit private

school providers have entered the market. Learning Alternatives, Inc., a creation of Minnesota businessman John Golle, is
gathering momentum. His Tesseract schools, though few in
number, are acquiring a track record, and Golle has recruited a
respected public school superintendent, David Bennett, who
started the Saturn school in St. Paul, as president.

Third, a growing number of private schools are designed to
serve the needs and interests of poor and limited-income minority parents. Found largely in the nation's bigger cities, they are in
rural areas as well. While their number is limited to several
hundred at present, they are viewed by civil rights advocate
Robert Woodson, founder of the National Center for Neighborhood Enterprise, as a key element in rebuilding distressed communities. Woodson sees effective private schools as a central part
of community building, representing an opportunity for local
citizens to build their own institutions.

Fourth, home schooling, a movement that was only weakly
developed five years ago, is becoming stronger. While home
schooling is not likely to enroll very large numbers of children, it
is an important movement for what it represents as much as for
what it does. It is above all a statement of profound dissatisfaction with the contemporary public school. Many home schoolers
are, to be sure, religious fundamentalists, who find modern secular life—not just schooling—repugnant. But increasing numbers
of parents—public school teachers among them—are turning to
home schooling as an intellectual alternative.

Once anathema to public school educators, home schooling
is recognized in some communities as a legitimate alternative to
formal public schools. Writing in the *Wall Street Journal*, Larry
Uzzell reports that the Cupertino, California, school district
makes supplies and textbooks available to home schoolers who
participate in a program of regular contacts with and reports to
the local public school—even though the home students never
attend. Home schooling offers a fascinating commentary on
modern life. The demands and opportunities of the modern,
high-tech, service economy are such that inventive families can
provide home schooling *and* income. Mom and Dad can both work
and teach their children at home because the modern workplace

has become so flexible. But they may also do so, at least in part, because the same technology that opens up new work horizons also makes it possible to "home school" more easily and effectively.

Indeed, it is no longer a matter of pure science fiction to imagine the school of the future as a state of mind and set of activities, rather than a brick and mortar structure.

Fifth, real models of real success now exist in the private sector that the public sector could not only emulate, but copy outright. In the first edition we described the Beacon Day School in Oakland, California. To paraphrase Dr. Johnson, we were as impressed that it existed at all as that it did well. Three years later the tantalizing success story of Beacon is now solidly rooted in accomplishment. Featured on "David Brinkley's Journal" in May 1991 as an example of the school of the future, it serves a heterogeneous population, including special education children, at less cost than most public schools, and it enjoys the loyalty of devoted parents and students.

And it is a New American School in every way, not just because it offers a developmental arts curriculum; or because it meets year round (240 days for students, 261 for faculty); or because Beacon has an extended day. Beacon is new to its core.

Let one example suffice. The faculty includes five "flex timers," members of the permanent staff who rotate among classes to cover for absent faculty members, teachers who are ill, receiving training, or on vacation. There are no itinerant substitutes at Beacon. More important, Beacon teachers rarely use sick leave, because the teachers themselves make all scheduling decisions, including vacation allocations. Contrast this to our major urban districts where "sick leave" is treated as "earned time off," creating teacher absenteeism almost as high as student absenteeism.

Sixth, the boundaries of public and private have begun to blur in the school world. Once the typical school's staff offered its full range of programs. Alternatives now abound. Just as a school may hire a private contractor to serve meals, drive buses, or trim lawns, so too a school may hire education service delivery from the private sector. For example, Berlitz, the famous private language school, is available for contract services to provide language instruction.

Seventh, if private and public boundaries are becoming indistinct in these areas, consider for-profit education. ARA Services, Kindercare, and Jostens Learning are just a few of the major players with the resources, experience, and interest to enter the field in a big way. Whittle Communications has already attracted attention with the introduction of Channel One, a commercial, for-profit TV channel—with advertising—broadcast directly to schools. Whittle's recently announced plan to design the new American school, from the ground up, and launch a national system of for-profit schools, is unprecedented in its daring and boldness. (It is not, of course, connected with the New American School plan announced by the president and the secretary of education.)

Historically, for-profit education at any level in American life has been a small part of the story. Indeed, of the more than 23,000 private elementary and secondary schools, only a few hundred are for-profit. And while the numbers are larger at the postsecondary level, for-profit providers are the exception, not the rule. Indeed, there are none among schools of the first rank. Why?

There is no definitive answer, but the reasons are not hard to fathom. Historically, education has never been thought of as a "money maker," an enterprise that might attract and hold entrepreneurs. To the contrary, the education enterprise has always been conservative—not politically, but socially and culturally. Education and entrepreneurship did not mix. Thus, quite naturally, education grew in a not-for-profit environment.

Perhaps most telling, however, is the fact that education—labor-intensive in the extreme—has had little profit potential. To be not-for-profit, then, simply "reconciled freedom with necessity," to use Nietzsche's memorable phrase.

And once established, and protected by a deftly woven legislative skein of protection for not-for-profits, schools found the circumstance congenial: no business licenses needed; no income taxes or other taxes on "profit," sales, or property; no dividends to pay; tax sheltering for gifts and bequests from friends and alumni; simple books to keep. And there are no serious limitations on what employees—or founders—can take out in the way of salaries and perquisites. A substantial salary, an expense account, a car, first-class travel to meetings and conventions in watering spots, membership in clubs. Indeed, the closer one looks, the more nearly the not-for-profit world looks like the for-profit world, without the nuisances. In not-for-profits with substantial income streams, the participants suffer not a whit.

The only thing not-for-profits miss is the opportunity to reap huge returns—if huge returns are to be had. But to date there is no educational equivalent of the high-flying, successful corporation, whose equity increases dramatically.

A school's wealth is measured in "human" not physical capital; there is little "equity" in a conventional sense. Indeed the closest thing to a school—in economic terms—would be a professional partnership or corporation in which partners own the "good will" their participation produces.

Yet suddenly, with a rush, for-profit schools are the subject of intense interest. Why? Because times have changed. In two important ways. First, technology. Finally there is real promise of breakthrough. Look for a moment at the history of education. First there was the tutorial and small lecture, from Socrates to royal tutors. Mass education was made possible by the development of a modern technology, the mass-produced textbook. But in most other respects, education remains unchanged. Indeed, it is the most obdurate of our social institutions.

Whoever unlocks the secrets of education technology, whoever devises major productivity increases, stands on the threshold of enormous wealth for one simple reason: Knowledge is power. The demand for education will only increase. And while we know this to be true, while we know the foundations of the modern economy are knowledge-based, while we know that in the late twentieth century human capital is more important than physical capital, we do not yet have the technologies at our disposal to create human capital as readily as we create physical capital. But at some point we will.

Why is this important? It will break the mold, eliminate the labor-intensive gridlock. That is the promise of technology in every field. It makes high volume and high quality possible, thereby reducing unit cost. Public schools, as they are currently

organized, have no incentive to either create or use such techno-
logical breakthroughs. Indeed, they have no more interest in
technology than the medieval guilds did. And like the Luddites
of the nineteenth century, schools are actively afraid of, even
hostile to, technology, because in their bones educators know
that technology will replace people. It always has, it always will.
And educators' hunches and fears are justified.

But few recognize that as technology eliminates labor—as
technology substitutes physical capital for human capital—it also
creates demand, upstream and downstream, for more human
capital. It creates wealth, which increases aggregate demand, as
well as supply. Thus, the long-term promise of education technology is more, not less, education, at lower unit costs.

And that is why the entry of for-profit firms into education is
so powerful and potentially important—finally there are players
with the financial incentive to do what is needed. While it is too
early to predict whether they will be successful, one thing is clear:
Someone will make the breakthrough. It is just a matter of time.

*   *   *   *

We are content with the recommendations we made in the
first edition of *Winning the Brain Race*, but what omissions and
oversights did we commit? To my mind there are several, and
they deserve brief comment. We said little about early childhood
education, although we recognize that becoming an educated
person is a seamless web. Education does not begin with kinder-
garten and end with postgraduate study; it begins before conception with maternal health and ends only with death. Elementary
and secondary education is merely a conspicuous part of a much
longer process. Society must reach out in the early years to provide opportunities, especially for the disadvantaged and dispossessed, to prepare for formal schooling.

The prestigious Committee for Economic Development
(CED) in its policy statements (*Investing in Our Children: Business
and the Public Schools, Children in Need: Investment Strategies for the
Educationally Disadvantaged,* and *The Unfinished Agenda: A New
Vision for Child Development and Education*) have fully examined
this problem—and this opportunity. We could add little to these

thoughtful statements in this short book; at this point we merely wish to reaffirm their findings and recommendations.

We are also convinced that we must go beyond the CED statements to a fundamental and necessary transformation in public elementary and secondary education—private school choice. To be more precise, the education of the public is the public's business, but I do not believe that American youngsters should be restricted to those schools owned and operated by government.

Although in the first edition we supported public school choice only, I believe that parents and children should have the opportunity to attend private schools—at public expense—in certain circumstances. The "right" to attend private schools is already enshrined in law in *Pierce* v. *Society of Sisters*, an Oregon case from the 1920s, in which the U.S. Supreme Court ruled that the state could not force children to satisfy the compulsory attendance law in public school only. It is time to extend this right to poor children, who now may have the legal right to attend religious schools but do not have the means. Enter Title I, the most important single program of the Johnson administration's federal role for education.

Its purpose and design were simple—to provide extra financial resources for the education of poor youngsters. Title I (now Chapter 1) is the logical and defensible extension of collateral social programs—in health care, housing, transportation, and higher education—in which the state helps those in need.

The idea, which seems so obvious and reasonable today, raised a firestorm of controversy in the early 1960s. Indeed, the very notion of a federal role in education was controversial, and it took all of President Lyndon B. Johnson's legendary powers of persuasion to get the Elementary and Secondary Education Act of 1965 (ESEA) enacted. One special bit of wizardry was also required. Direct aid to elementary and secondary age students had not been enacted in the preceding century and a half because of deep divisions about aid to religious schools. To overstate the case only slightly, non-Catholics were afraid that public support from Washington would lead to aid to Catholic schools. Catholics, on the other hand, were afraid that public aid would not flow to Catholic schools, leaving them more isolated than ever.

At the same time there was a growing conviction that aid to the poor was essential if the education of the poor were to be improved. Johnson's genius was to tie the two ideas together, and with a promise of aid to all poor children—whether they attended public or parochial school—he was able to marshal the necessary votes for ESEA. He needed the votes of big-city Democrats, and this artful compromise delivered them.

ESEA was a landmark, for both its accomplishments and the stable relationships it created over time. The divisive and difficult relationship between public and religious schools became a harmonious and smooth one. It took time, but it worked.

Enter the U.S. Supreme Court. In *Aguilar* v. *Felton* (1985) the court struck down a program with a twenty-year history of success and overturned the practice whereby poor youngsters could receive Title I services in parochial schools .

The swing vote was cast by Justice Lewis F. Powell, Jr., who was painfully aware of the problem created by *Aguilar*. A narrow constitutional interpretation destroyed a commendable program to aid to poor children; their need was manifest, the quality of their programs high, their only legal sin was to exercise their religious beliefs and attend religious schools. Recognizing the fundamental inequity in the case, Powell invited Congress to fashion a constitutionally defensible program, one that would not breach the tradition of separation of church and state. In effect, he invited Congress to devise a Chapter 1 voucher scheme. In his concurring opinion, Powell said:

> The court has never foreclosed the possibility that some types of aid to parochial schools could be valid under the Establishment Clause. . . . If, for example, the Congress could fashion a program of evenhanded financial assistance to both public and private schools that could be administered, with governmental supervision in the private schools, so as to prevent the diverson of the aid from secular purposes, we would be presented with a different question.

Congress has not yet done this, in large measure because the public schools—those that benefited most from ESEA twenty-five years ago—refused to come to the aid of their former allies, the religious schools that had been the keystone of the original Chapter 1 compromise of 1965. Once again Catholic and other religious schools that served the poor were friendless and alone. And the victims were—are—poor children whose families are prepared to sacrifice to send them to religiously affiliated schools.

In a structurally similar case, *Bowen* v. *Roy*, the plaintiff, Little Bird of the Snow, an American Indian child, was denied AFDC (Aid to Families with Dependent Children) benefits because her parents would not secure a social security number for her. Her parents believed that a number would "rob" Little Bird of her "spirit" and violate her religious liberty. The Court found that,

> While an individual may not compel the government to act in accordance with his religious beliefs, neither as a general rule may the government require that an individual breach a religious precept in order to avoid losing governmental benefits to which he would be otherwise entitled.

Yet *Aguilar* does precisely this. It requires children who need and are otherwise entitled to federally funded speech and testing services and remedial education programs in reading, language, or mathematics either to enroll in public school—forsaking their religious preferences—or to benefit from those special services outside the religious school premises in a setting acceptable to the government.

Unhappily, moral and ethical arguments carry little weight in the education community, and simple equity appears not to be a strong enough argument on behalf of youngsters who wish to attend religious schools. Perhaps an instrumental argument will do the job.

Since the original enactment of ESEA, another important event unfolded, the research of the eminent sociologist James Coleman. Not surprisingly, his research found that poor youngsters do better—by a significant margin—in inner-city Catholic schools than they do in public schools. The issue, then, is no longer an abstract one of moral justice, but a practical matter with the most important consequences.

Confronted by a dreadful problem of low academic achievement by poor youngsters across the country, we have at our disposal a known policy remedy—vouchers to attend privately organized and operated schools that work. These are not elite institutions, neither are they "white flight" or "bright flight" schools—they are humble parish schools, racially and socially integrated, serving high public purposes.

In almost any other social policy area—in housing, health, welfare, criminal justice, transportation, or nutrition—Congress would rush to enact such an obvious and effective remedy. But Congress has refused to move with Chapter 1 vouchers because the public schools have resisted this system. Public school reluctance to support private schools is particularly disappointing because Title I exists in the first instance because of their common cause with Catholic schools; and now poor children are denied a proven remedy when their need is greater than ever.

The courts, uncertain allies in the push for school reform and renewal, could enter the fray under the terms of a suit now pending in Kansas City. Plaintiffs are poor children—mostly but not exclusively black—who correctly argue that the public schools are not providing an adequate education. Nor are they likely to. The remedy they seek is simplicity itself: Have the Kansas City school district make available to these poor children some of the financial resources that would otherwise be spent on their education in the form of vouchers to attend local private schools.

The seats are available. The private schools guarantee that. The education would, by any measure, be superior. The cost would be substantially less—the district would actually save significant amounts of money—and the children would be better off. Moreover, I am convinced that the public schools would also be better off, over the long haul. We do them no favor by sheltering them from the rigors of competition. Isolation from market forces has left them slack and enervated, unable to respond to the legitimate needs of their students and community.

I want to make one point forcefully. We and others have devoted much time and energy to explaining the importance of markets in education, particularly as seen from the demand side. Indeed, there is much to be said about markets as they respond to the needs and interests of consumers. But demand is only half the story.

The other half, equally important, is supply—the role that providers play in markets. In education, the most important part of the supply side is teachers. What is in it for them? Everything, we believe, for a focus on the supply side of the market will permit them to emerge from the shadows of the bureaucracy and become professionals.

Think of consumer sovereignty in other areas. Are lawyers, architects, accountants, and doctors passive victims who are exploited by rapacious consumers? Are they at a disadvantage because they are in the market? Do their private sector salaries suffer in comparison to their counterparts in the public sector? Do lawyers make more money as district attorneys or judges or as corporation counsels?

We all know the answer. The private sector satisfies the interests of professionals precisely because they are able to offer their services competitively. Indeed, their professionalism, special knowledge, skills, and abilities put them in a favored position. The consumer is buying the professional's knowledge and expertise. The professional is not at the mercy of the client, but neither is the client at the mercy of the professional.

Are there any losers in this scenario? Indeed there are—middle managers who refuse to meet their obligations to workers (teachers) and customers (students and their families). Markets do not exist for the convenience of owners and managers. To the contrary, the purpose of a market is to put heat on owners and managers, to make them perform. That is what markets are all about.

*   *   *   *

Since the first edition of this book, much has happened. There have been triumphs as well as disappointments in education. Two of the school superintendents we extolled—Eugene Reveille of Rochester and Richard Green, then of Minneapolis and subsequently superintendent of the New York City schools—have died. They were men of vision and accomplishment, and their loss is keenly felt.

On a happier note, two superintendents whose leadership and accomplishments we extolled have gone on to even greater accomplishments. Joseph Fernandez continued to transform Miami-Dade schools until he was lured away by New York City to take on perhaps the toughest school assignment in the nation. If anyone can make New York City schools work, Joe Fernandez can.

And John Murphy, architect of massive and lasting reform in Prince George's County, Maryland, has been hired by the large and important Charlotte-Mecklenburg district in North Carolina to oversee a period of important transition. He will be an asset to this school system with promise.

The Rochester, New York, district appears to be in deep trouble, reform as much a memory as a promise. Does this mean they failed? I don't think so. It is a sign they set their sights high and took the risks that were necessary, even if they were not sufficient. As Al Shanker of the American Federation of Teachers notes wryly, the problem with education research is that "all education experiments are doomed to succeed." Rochester's "failure"—if indeed it turns out to be a failure—should help us all learn about the process of lasting school reform. This seems a stern discipline in the public sector, but it is necessary; in the high-tech world we learn as much from our failures as from our successes and so too should we in education.

I conclude this new chapter, then, with comments on what I have learned in the past few years, what we neglected to note in the first edition, and where we go from here.

Some of the ideas we originally proposed are being taken seriously, both in the foundation world and among real schools with real students. Both of us served on the advisory board of the RJR Nabisco Foundation's Next Century Schools program, and the experience was invaluable. The idea of foundation chairman (and RJR Nabisco CEO) Lou Gerstner and foundation president Roger Semerad, Next Century Schools is "venture capital" for teachers and principals.

Three-year grants of up to $750,000 are available to as many as fifteen schools a year to design and implement bold and entrepreneurial school reform and restructuring. Public-sector educational venture capital was an idea we developed in the first edition, where we urged the federal government to provide up to $40 million per year for the nation's schools. A bold program, but one that is still unfulfilled. It took the leadership of the RJR Nabisco Foundation to make it a reality, at a funding level without precedent in the private sector.

Now in its second round of grants, Next Century Schools has made awards to thirty schools across the country, ranging from impoverished rural and inner-city schools to affluent suburban districts. The power of the program is its utter simplicity and directness—it is a vote of confidence in the wit and wisdom of the nation's front-line education troops, the teachers and principals who do the work. Teachers and principals at the school building level—not the school district—with a dream and a vision are invited to submit a ten-page prospectus, laying out what they would like to do, how they will do it, what it will cost, and why they think they will succeed.

What have I learned from this process? A number of things, not the least of which is that the RJR Nabisco Foundation's idea is sound; there is a pressing need for "education venture capital." Our schools are on a short leash, denied the creativity and imagination that teachers and principals can bring to the undertaking we call "schooling." Like their students, they are the victims of bureaucracy; their professional lives are circumscribed by an outmoded system of education, one that treats teachers like blue collar workers of the early industrial era. Indeed, in many respects, today's teachers are not treated as well as modern blue collar workers; in today's corporation, the blue collar worker is expected to take the initiative, to solve problems, to work in teams—in short, to do those things many managers once thought were the exclusive province of professionals.

Fortune magazine highlighted the issue in a spring 1991 cover story entitled "Workers without Bosses." Indeed, the issue is more than "workers without bosses"—it is workers as their own bosses, working collaboratively and collegially, as professionals do.

How do I know that Next Century Schools is on the right track? One certain sign will be a shock to most educators, even most members of the public, but it will be no surprise to the high-tech community. What is it? One major winner has failed utterly; their winning proposal was fully funded at $750,000, but they were not able to get their program under way within the terms of the grant. As a consequence, they have forfeited the funds and missed a historic opportunity to create an education vision. But what does their failure really mean? They set their sights too high; they misjudged the degree of difficulty they would encounter; they misperceived the political environment in which they would operate. But they also offered a potent lesson to us all; their failure has taught us as much as their success would have. The bitter truth is that many schools confront a hostile bureaucratic and political environment, and the barriers to change are numerous and difficult to overcome.

There are internal, self-reinforcing barriers to change as well. Many principals and teachers are hesitant about or even fearful of change. This hesitancy emerged early on, and I dubbed it the "Elsa the lion syndrome." Remember Elsa, the heroine of the splendid movie, *Born Free*? Raised in captivity, she is eventually to be let free in the wild. She is taken to the veld and her cage door opened—and she will not budge. She stays put, thank you very much. The wild may be fine for some lions, but not Elsa. At least not at first.

Many of the proposals submitted to Next Century Schools were like Elsa—afraid, at first, to venture into the wild. Why? Teachers and principals aren't dummies, particularly Next Century School winners. And although they were risk takers, they were careful. They know the rules, they know the system of incentives and disincentives at work in the public sector. And they weren't going to rock the boat. At least not in obvious ways that would bring them to the attention of people who disapprove of boat rocking. They are the "canny outlaws" to whom we have referred, men and women who know how to get things done, and know that the best way to do so is behind closed doors.

Next Century Schools and other programs like it may permit—even encourage—more and more teachers and principals to come out of the bureaucratic closet, to act like professionals and be proud of it.

Next Century Schools will inspire imitators—the sincerest

form of flattery—that, after all, is one of the prime reasons for private philanthropy, to step in and do those things the public sector should do but doesn't yet have the nerve or knowledge to get under way. So too will Ted Sizer's Essential Schools, James Comer's Effective Schools, Burger King's academies, Bill Millikin's Cities in Schools, the American Express academies, Henry Levin's Accelerated Schools, the St. Paul, Minnesota, Saturn school, and others like these across the country.

These schools are appearing on the scene because they are necessary. Someone must invent the school of tomorrow. And that is why Secretary Alexander, with President Bush's active support, has proposed the New American School, of which one—at least—will be funded in every congressional district in the nation.

Inventing or creating or discovering the "new" idea is a staple of the modern world of high technology, but it is still a mystery to most school districts. Indeed, it is hard to imagine a more conservative enterprise than schooling. Virtually unchanged for centuries, schools have been resistant to modernization for as long as we can remember. Not only do schools labor under an archaic organizational form—modeled on the factory of the late nineteenth and early twentieth century—but schools march to the farm's drumbeat. Imagine, an agrarian calendar in the late twentieth century, when fewer than 3 percent of the nation lives on the land.

Indeed, of all the predictions that can be made about the school of the future, only one can be made with confidence—that we won't recognize it. It will serve the same function—educating children—but it will be as different as the automobile and the carriage. True, the automobile was first the "horseless carriage," but its full development was stalled so long as designers worked with blinders on. The horseless carriage was only a phase, though perhaps a necessary one.

Consider, as well, the difference between a candle and a light bulb; they serve similar functions, but in appearance and operation they are as different from one other as can be. When the revolution in the schools is under way, they may not be recognizable either. The kind of change we call for will revolutionize not just school input and output, but to use the jargon of computers, school "throughput." The introduction of technology, for instance, when it is finally successful, will transform schools. Or perhaps more to the point, schools must be transformed to use technology wisely and well.

As I noted earlier, in all other areas of modern life technology is viewed as a labor saver, a productivity enhancer, a device to get more output for a given unit of input. That is why the farmer moves from a mule and plow to a tractor, why the journalist abandons his cherished upright typewriter for a laptop, why an office uses copiers instead of carbon paper or offset printing. In each case substantial productivity increases occur, costs are reduced, labor is saved, conditions of work are improved, and morale goes up. And wonder of wonders, the technology is self-liquidating. It not only pays for itself, and returns a profit, it sets the stage for its own obsolescence and the creation of other new technologies.

What else does technology do? It changes every single relationship in the organization, the tried and true and the cherished. It changes the pattern and pace of work and interoffice communication; it changes rewards and penalties, incentives and disincentives. It exposes everyone in the organization to potential—and sometimes actual—embarrassment, even humiliation. To overcome these formidable barriers, the power of technology, its promise and delivery, must be immense—as it is in businesses that use technology.

British newspapers were not merely slow to adopt modern production technologies, they were positively obdurate. Only hard reality could force them to do so. Only when the *Wall Street Journal*, printed abroad with the latest in production technologies, began to appear on London streets *before* British dailies did Fleet Street recognize that it was time to modernize.

A failure to come to terms with this aspect of technology explains the schools' antediluvian performance. Most educators see technology as bells and whistles, treating it as most of us do a radio in a new car—it doesn't affect performance or direction, it just makes getting there more pleasant. That's why most schools use technology as a costly add-on, not a labor- and money-saving substitution. Educators across the nation assert that they do not have the money for technology.

They are looking at the problem exactly backwards—they can't afford not to use technology. Indeed, if our schools are to succeed, educators must be educated in this area above all. Technology has one purpose—to enhance productivity. And its effective use will transform not just what a school accomplishes, but how it accomplishes it.

Think for a moment about a $220 billion industry, one that consumes 7 percent of GNP and is still in the technological dark ages. As the mass-produced textbook made modern mass education possible, so too computers will eventually make high-quality mass education possible.

John Murphy is one of the few educators in the country who understands both the transforming and cost-saving implications of technology. He introduced computers in Prince George's County schools as a savings, not an expenditure. True, there were unusual, one-time, up-front costs—the district had to pay for the new technology. But it did so by taking a five-year loan at commercial rates and repaying it out of future labor savings.

Luckily for Murphy, the school district, and the teachers' unions, the labor saving was not achieved through firings or RIFs ("reductions in force," to use the government euphemism), but through forgone hiring. Workers who would otherwise have been hired were not, and the budgeted amounts were made available to invest in technology. I use the word *invest* advisedly, for technology is an investment. Technology is not just fun, though it often is that; technology is not just cost-effective, though it must be if it is to be justified. Technology is a commitment to doing things differently and better.

This anecdote from the trenches is unusual in the world of public education, yet it must become the norm if public schooling is to survive. We must not lose sight of one implication of technology—that as long as schools are run as labor-intensive assembly lines, pay and conditions of work will never be what they should be. Teachers must understand that their long-term self-interest is served by investing in technology, reorganizing the profession, and turning teachers into "managers" of instruction.

This has happened in industry. Look at Volvo, the Swedish automobile manufacturer. Pioneer of worker participation and shared decision making, Volvo now defines the role of manager as "manager as teacher," the simple reverse of our formulation, "teacher as manager of instruction." This difference is no accident.

A final note on technology is in order. How is it possible for the Japanese to achieve so much with low-tech schools? A fair question. Let me answer with an example. Remember the introduction of the automated teller machine (ATM)? The rollout was nearly a disaster. Instead of offering the ATM as a convenience, the banks told customers they *had* to use it; the privilege of dealing with a human teller would be reserved for big customers. Why was this a problem? Most customers hated ATMs in the beginning because they were forced to use them. It was confusing, intimidating, and even embarrassing (when you couldn't make it work in front of a long line of impatient people).

And at an intuitive level, the customer understood the secret of the ATM's appeal to financial institutions: The ATM makes the customer do the work. With an ATM you are your own teller. The ATM is to banking what fast food is to traditional restaurants—you stand in line, serve yourself, and seat yourself. You're even encouraged to pick up after yourself. The mixture of high volume and self-service represents a major saving to the provider, but the customer will use it only if it provides real benefits.

What does the ATM provide the customer? Escape from the confines of banking hours and bureaucracy. And now, after ten years, the ATM provides virtually universal access, twenty-four hours a day, to banking services around the country and the world.

What does this example have to do with Japanese schools and their extraordinarily high output? It's the same formula at work: The customers do the work while the school enjoys high volume. Japanese students work like galley slaves, they never complain or act up, the "service" (curriculum and tests) the schools offer is as uniform as our national ATM network, and the Japanese have among the highest student-faculty ratios in the world—forty-two students per teacher is the norm.

If the low-tech, labor-intensive Japanese example gives you solace, just wait until Japanese schools go high tech. It will be revolutionary.

And as every reader knows, yesterday's revolutionary idea is today's accepted practice. The concept of choice, for example, was radical a decade ago, was "leading edge" when the first edition of this book was released, and is now widely accepted and practiced. We have talked about its benefits to consumers and have argued that in many respects the impact of choice will be greater and more satisfying to providers. A final and truly radical word on choice: I propose to end compulsory attendance. Children should not be required by law to attend school after the fourteenth birthday.

How could I possibly suggest throwing out compulsory attendance, which is viewed by many as a triumph of progressive reform? The hard fact is that compulsory attendance doesn't work and no longer makes sense. It is a symbol of an archaic era, that of the "administered" school. In the modern era school should not be compulsory any more than the military should— not because school is unimportant, but because it is so important that no one can do without it. School doesn't have to be compulsory. (A recommendation of this kind is clearly so radical that few government officials would be likely to support it.)

To the contrary, school should be viewed as an opportunity, an oasis, a place one *wants* to go, not where one *must* go. Instead of requiring attendance, the state should guarantee access to all students, young and old, immigrant and native born. In a modern democracy, all citizens should enjoy the right to a free education, one that will lead to a high school diploma of some distinction, at whatever age and in whatever set of circumstances they are ready to secure it. If you want to drop out and flip hamburgers for a while, so be it, but you should be guaranteed the right to return when you're ready—when you've learned your lesson. Schools should not be babysitting institutions for the unmotivated or disaffected.

The dropout who returns to school—as return he must— need not return to a conventional public school, a building full of classrooms, classrooms full of desks. The dropout, or the adult immigrant, or the semiliterate native-born student who seeks a high school diploma can enroll in a computerized "store front" school, can take courses by broadcast T.V., can check out a VCR or CD learning sequence, can attend a private training facility in the evening or on weekends—or both. The only limit is the imagination.

This practical yet visionary observation brings us full circle, for the school of the future must abandon the organizational rigidities of the present. We can no longer afford a factory model school, in which the student is the product, the teacher the worker. As we have suggested, in the school of the future the teacher must be the manager of instruction, and the student the worker. The product is education. It can be no other way. Education is not a passive process of pouring facts and attitudes into an empty vessel; it is an active, dynamic, interactive process, in which students learn not just because they have good teachers, but because they are motivated, they are part of the team. In the final analysis we must all accept responsibility for education; we must choose our future.

2

Choice, Consumer Sovereignty, and the Education Marketplace

There is nothing more basic to education and its ability to bring our children into the 21st century than choice. Given a choice in public education, we believe parents will play a stronger role in our schools. Innovative programs will spring to life. Parents and the whole community will become more deeply involved in helping all children learn. Teachers will be more challenged than ever. And, most importantly, our students will see immediate results.
—The National Governors' Association
Time for Results: The Governors'
1991 Report on Education

BY ANY MEASURE, today's educational system is a failed monopoly. That it is failing large numbers of students is beyond dispute—one quarter do not graduate and another quarter are so poorly prepared academically that they are not ready for work or postsecondary education. But does that unacceptably high rate of failure have anything to do with the schools' monopoly position? We are convinced it does. The monopolist is free to ignore the legitimate needs and interests of both the consumer and the worker, a picture that describes the reality of today's education system. Teachers and students are the losers.

With more than 15,500 nominally independent school districts across the nation, it's true that schools are not a monopoly in the classic sense economists use to describe monopoly in business. There is not a single, national provider. Nevertheless, each school district enjoys a monopoly position with its "consumers," the citizens who live within its boundaries. And the vast majority of school districts do not permit interdistrict transfers. In the parlance of business, that would be known as "conspiracy in restraint of trade." Like the teachers who work for the schools, the students and families who are their customers must accept what the educational bureaucracy deigns to offer.

The reason is not ill will or maliciousness, but the nature of monopoly provision—as power corrupts, absolute power corrupts absolutely. So, too, does centralized monopoly power. Whether that power is in state hands or private hands, the monopolist's privilege is to ignore workers and customers.

It is not surprising that businessmen who became successful monopolists enjoyed their monopolies. Indeed, who in the business world has not, in a weak moment, longed for a monopoly position? How it would simplify life to tell customers to take it or leave it, to set prices by fiat, to tell workers the terms of their employment. In one fell swoop, monopoly solves the thorny problems of competition and consumer sovereignty, and makes the owner king.

The fact is, business is no more virtuous than education, and could business leaders but take a monopoly position, many would—as many have—because the purpose of competition is to serve the consumer and not the producer, the worker and not the owner. Competition makes the manager work harder and provide better quality at lower cost to the consumer. And competition for workers makes the worker's life better, more interesting, and more lucrative, particularly in knowledge-intensive industries.

But if monopoly is to be disdained in the private sector, if it works to the disadvantage of the consumer in the economic realm, is there not a circumstance in which it is acceptable? Are there public goods or services that should be produced by only one provider? Surely the police power of the state fits this description, in both the domestic and international realms. Few would propose that national defense be contracted out to the lowest bidder, or that the local police be replaced with private *gendarmerie*. Is there a sense in which education fits this picture, a privileged activity that deserves an exclusive franchise?

The answer is "yes," if the purpose of education is to serve the state. The argument runs that opportunity to change schools, to improve them, is political, not economic. The public can vote for school boards, and presumably get what it wants. But school boards don't know any more about education than the parents who put them there, which is why we believe that relying exclusively on the political process will not improve the schools. What's more, it is wholly at variance with the other learned professions. Can you imagine running hospitals or law practices by majority vote of a fixed political jurisdiction?

Think of schools in economic terms, as purposeful organizational units staffed with willing professionals and support staffs and patronized by willing customers. An economic model of education is both more democratic and more responsive than a political model. The essence of democracy is choice, and this frame of reference permits the public to think about schools and deal with them constructively.

Public elementary and secondary schools sink to the lowest common denominator in the political process. Because they must be all things to all people, they lose their identity, their autonomy, and eventually, their integrity. It's no wonder that discerning parents, students, and even teachers find them less and less attractive.

As a matter of fact, public school teachers are twice as likely as the public at large to enroll their children in private schools. They are the experts in education, and they know what's good and what's not. In Michigan, a little more than 10 percent of the general public enroll their children in private schools. Among public school teachers, it's 20 percent. In Chicago, where

20 percent of the public uses private schools, nearly 50 percent of public school teachers do.

When public school teachers don't trust the system enough to use it for their own kids, it's no wonder that almost half the public school parents support vouchers or tax credits for public or private schools. We are convinced that such an approach is both unnecessary and unwise. Our public schools are a priceless national resource, and we must re-infuse them with their sense of democratic purpose. But to do so, they must change radically, and choice *among* public schools is the change we need. Choice would do more to improve the overall quality of public education than any other reform we know of. The National Governors' Association stated recently:

> If we first implement choice, true choice among public schools, we unlock the values of competition in the educational marketplace. Schools that compete for students, teachers, and dollars will, by virtue of the environment, make those changes that allow them to succeed. Schools will, in fact, set the pace, forcing Governors and other policymakers to keep up. If our children are to be competitive in the international marketplace—and we must be competitive in the international marketplace—then we must be competitive here at home. While there are many questions to answer, choice in the public schools is the deregulatory move needed to make schools more responsive

But choice in and of itself is an empty concept unless there are different options available among alternate providers. Henry Ford, for example, is reputed to have said that customers could have any color Ford they wanted so long as it was black. A real education choice system can be effective only if it leads to significant diversity among schools, and if it is backed by the capacity of parents, students, and teachers to make real decisions.

What's required in a real choice system, then, is resources—resources devoted to choice. In a choice system, the state would fund individual children, rather than individual schools or school districts. Money earmarked for education would reach the public school *only* when the student elected to enroll. The school would lose its guaranteed income, and it would be forced to provide offerings that met the needs and interests of the community it proposed to serve.

The idea, of course, is an old one. It is a market, in which willing buyers and sellers come together to deal with each other. Once again, we do not include private schools in this formulation—yet. It is true that in the other industrialized democracies, private schools of all kinds—religious and secular—receive public funds. We are not yet ready to propose such an idea. Frankly, we think competition among public schools will strengthen both the public and private systems. But unless public schools begin to behave more like private schools, the time will come when public support of private schools will be a reality in this country as well. The reason is not hard to understand. The middle class in all advanced nations is expert at getting what it wants, through subsidies, gifts, tax breaks, or grants. Middle-class people are the decision makers, the backbone of a complex society. And if they are denied access to good public schools, they will eventually insist that their choice of private schools be subsidized. Public schools still have time to reform, but the sand is running through the hourglass.

Some public schools recognize how severe the problem has become. Some are trying new ways to make their schools places where teachers want to work and that parents can trust. In 1987 the Dade County Public Schools of Greater Miami began a major experiment to cut red tape and "create a new management model for large urban school districts." As reported by the *New York Times*, then–Miami superintendent Joseph A. Fernandez said, "It's the classroom teachers who know what kids need. It's time to let them try things that they think will work." Thirty-two schools in the Miami area were turned over to teams that include parents and teachers. Patrick L. Turnillo, Jr., executive vice-president of the American Federation of Teachers, says, "This is our last shot at making our public schools work. Either we change our schools dramatically, or the public will look for some other alternative."

Choice in the public sector would establish an all-public "market" where pressures of supply and demand could be made to work as surely as they do in the private sector. The first step in the process is to have education funds—federal, state, and local—follow the students wherever they go. Students could then attend any school they wanted to, regardless of where they lived, and they'd bring the same education dollars with them, regardless of how much money their parents made. For the first time, poor families would have options only the affluent have today. Children with comparable needs would be funded equally—neighborhood tax rates would not apply. Children with special learning problems would get more money. We already do all that in higher education. There's no reason why we can't do it with public elementary and high schools.

Think what that would do. With schools competing for students, operating income would be directly related to the number of children enrolled, which directly relates to customer preference and service.

The school district could no longer claim to "run" the school building. The building, to use the language of business, would be the profit or cost center, and the building manager—the principal—together with the teachers, would make up the decision-making team. Schools themselves would develop their own distinctive pedagogical and academic personalities that would attract students and their families.

Not only is this a model drawn from the business world, it is drawn from the world of private schools as well. Only rarely are they part of huge bureaucratic systems, and even when they are—as in the case of diocesan elementary schools—there is a very light administrative hand on the reins. Catholic order high schools, for example, are well known for their independence and autonomy (we speak here of academic, not theological matters.)

Among private schools that are not part of a hierarchical church, autonomy and independence are even more pronounced, for precisely the reason a market approach would predict. They must be able to respond to demand rapidly, flexibly, and smoothly. That does not mean that they are prey to the fads and vicissitudes of the moment. No responsible supplier in the private sector tries to meet every whim of every prospective purchaser. The issue here is flexibility and responsiveness in the context of academic and administrative standards. By way of illustration, look at what private schools have done over the past two decades. As public school curriculums got progressively "softer" and began to offer nonacademic courses such as driver education, "bachelor living," and "power volleyball"—for credit—private schools refused to compromise. By and large, they didn't introduce a general track curriculum. They retained a heavy academic emphasis.

It is this reason—attention to academics—that explains higher test scores in private schools. Critics are quick to note that private schools are more selective with their student bodies, and that because religious schools are on tight budgets, they don't have the luxury of a broad range of course offerings. We would simply state that private schools exist in a market—a vigorous market—characterized by supply and demand. In the private sector, people get what they pay for. For the public sector to ignore that simple truth is folly.

One of the most important aspects of choice among schools will be a change in attitudes, between students and their families and between teachers and the larger school community. A sense of reciprocity and mutuality will be created, as it is in other professions. Doctors and lawyers, for example, respect their clients, and their clients have confidence in them, because the relationship is voluntary.

Choice—voluntary association and voluntary commerce—is the essence of the successful modern company, as well. Although the technical foundation of Xerox's success is xerography, Xerox's long-term success is due to Xerox's conviction that the customer is king. That is not an idle platitude, but the foundation stone of Xerox's corporate philosophy. A corporation that ignores that simple truth is doomed. A consumer-oriented company can slip for only a very short time before consumer dissatisfaction shows up in the ledger as a loss statement. Xerox is constantly on the alert for signs of consumer satisfaction and dissatisfaction. To do otherwise is suicidal for any contemporary business.

Xerox relies on one additional means of staying responsive. Everyone in senior management, from the CEO on down, spends one day a month receiving phone calls from customers.

Xerox senior managers also talk regularly to customers in the field. There is simply no substitute for direct access. It keeps managers informed, it keeps them in touch, it keeps them honest.

Is there a lesson in this for schools? We believe there is, because just as voluntary choice works for business, it can work for education. We have talked at some length about customer satisfaction, because we believe every service organization must stress it, and must be forced to deliver or pay the price of failure. A captive audience simply rewards failure, and permits unhealthy practices to continue and become institutionalized.

It's important to remember that business would not escape this fate if choice and competition didn't exist. Business is not inherently more virtuous or clever than the schools, nor are business leaders necessarily better educated or connected than educational leaders. In business, it's sink or swim, satisfy the customer or go out of business. It's not superior virtue that drives business—it's necessity. Without the discipline of competition, organizations begin to serve their managers and owners, rather than their customers. It's an iron rule, because people throughout history, across cultures, and across institutions prefer the easy to the difficult path. Competition makes business perform. It can make schools perform.

There are two sides to the coin of choice. Once a student has voluntarily chosen a school, he or she is an accomplice, a partner, a participant. Just as the student/customer can expect the school to do what it promised when it encouraged students to enroll in the first place, the school can expect the student to meet its standards. That's true in the business world, as well.

Choice in business does not mean offering a vast array of products. And while overspecialization can be a danger, the bigger danger for most corporations is trying to do too many things. Successful corporations occupy well-defined niches in the business world, in precisely the way successful flora and fauna occupy ecological niches in the natural world.

Xerox believes in doing a few things very well—Xerox's business is people, helping them to communicate in the modern, global economy. As a consequence, there are large segments of modern markets that hold no interest for Xerox and large numbers of people who will never be Xerox customers. Xerox is convinced that the product line it offers is the right one.

Choice among schools is precisely analogous. Students and their families who choose a school do so in large measure because it is sharply focused, not because it tries to be all things to all people. Indeed, among schools of choice already in existence, that's exactly what happens. In New York City, for example, where schools of choice have been a reality for decades, significant market differentiation exists. The Bronx High School of Science offers one curriculum; Manhattan's High School of the Performing Arts another; Aviation in Queens yet another; and Murry Bergtraum in lower Manhattan another.

In the private school world where choice is the byword, variety and diversity are breathtaking. There are religiously affiliated schools with a range as diverse as the religious communities from which they are drawn: Hebrew, Catholic, Lutheran, Seventh Day Adventist, Episcopal, Quaker. Even within denominations, there are significant differences—Catholic order schools differ one from the other, with Benedictine, Christian Brothers, and Jesuit schools having distinctive personalities.

One of the most fascinating developments of the past three decades has been the explosive growth of black, non-Catholic enrollment in urban Catholic schools. Black working and middle-class Protestants—largely Baptists, who ordinarily have little affinity for Catholicism—enroll their children in Catholic schools, because they see them as an affordable option, a choice that meets their educational needs.

The role of private schools in modern American society offers another interesting commentary on how a large-scale choice system could be expected to work in the public sector. The conventional wisdom has it that private schools have an easier time of it, because they can expel students more easily than public schools.

The facts, however, are just the contrary—private schools rarely expel youngsters, precisely because they can. To educators, that may sound ironic, even incomprehensible, but not to business people. The freedom to act in a certain way is itself a powerful stimulus to change behavior. As a consequence, expulsion or firing for cause only rarely takes place.

If the student has chosen the school in the first instance, he has a reasonably strong incentive to stay, or failing that, to choose another school that will satisfy his interests. This is not just a matter of explicit threats—throwing the fear of God into an employee or student—though on occasion it may involve that. What is more important is the implicit understanding on both sides of the desk that both parties are stakeholders, and both have an interest in working together cooperatively and effectively.

As the economist Peter Drucker observes, "If I've put a person into a job and he or she doesn't perform, I've made a mistake." The manager's job is to manage, the teacher's job is to teach. Only in a monopoly can you get away with blaming the victim. One of the major insights of modern management theory has to do with employee "fit"—an employee who may be wonderful in one environment may not function in another. If the "fit" is poor, as Drucker says, the executive must admit "I made a mistake, and it's my job to correct it. To keep people in a job they can't do isn't being kind—it's being cruel."

Choice should be especially promising for teachers and administrators. No longer would they view themselves as wardens and guards; they would reassume their rightful role as educators. With choice systems in place, elementary and secondary school educators could expect to be treated much the way college and university faculties are, with greater respect and affection.

One aspect of choice systems that deserves special note is the beneficial impact it could have on the underclass we see emerging in many of our central cities. This new underclass, which many analysts fear is a permanent underclass, is frequently trapped in intergenerational poverty, with only a casual attachment to the labor force and little or no contact with mainstream America. We are convinced that this underclass must be helped to strengthen indigenous community resources and to gain access to other social resources not now available in their communities. The single most important resource these people need is access to schools that serve their needs. By that we mean not only schools that offer a full array of ancillary services, such as health clinics and day care, but schools that are community-based, schools that can expect to modify the *social* as well as the academic behavior of their students.

The Committee for Economic Development's policy statement, *Investing in Our Children: Business and the Public Schools*, draws a powerfully important distinction that bears on this point. The policy statement says that there are basically two curriculums, a "visible" curriculum and an "invisible" curriculum. The visible curriculum is the part of the school that stresses academic content and accomplishment. The invisible curriculum communicates attitudes and information about acceptable and appropriate behavior. Youngsters today must master both. They need to be able to read and write, as well as meet the public and interact effectively.

Indeed, that is one of the important lessons of the service economy that is too often ignored. Not only is the service economy "knowledge-based" in terms of content, its setting is highly interactive in terms of human contact. Pick and shovel work is fairly solitary. But service work is people-oriented and requires significant social skills. Imagine the social skills any corporate employee needs to interact with a wide variety of people, colleagues, subordinates, superiors, customers, members of the public generally. Those social skills are so widely diffused through the middle class that most of us take them for granted, but their absence spells unemployability.

Most youngsters acquire those skills, first at home, and only secondarily at school. Schools reinforce them and support them, but it is difficult for schools to impart them whole cloth except in special circumstances. Without exception, part of the appeal of religiously affiliated schools is precisely that they build character and impart strong lessons about behavior and attitudes. We are not proposing that the underclass be assigned to religious schools—though insofar as they prefer to go to them, the idea is a sound one. Rather, we think that schools of choice will have significantly more maneuvering room in such sensitive areas as the "invisible" curriculum. A school—particularly a public school—may more easily require uniform dress, codes of deportment, punctuality, homework, and civility if it is a school the student chooses to attend.

That suggests to us that with schools of choice, there will be a special role for "mediating structures," the term coined by Peter Berger and John Neuhaus in their important book *To Empower People*. They mean the voluntary, fraternal, and benevolent associations by which most of us tend to define ourselves. Those are nongovernment forms of association—churches and synagogues, unions, clubs, political parties, voluntary meetings, community groups, lodges, in all the remarkable variety that exists in this country. So important are they that they are the first place people turn in time of need. They have a powerfully important role to play in education choice systems.

What will the nature of this role be? Using the business metaphor that runs throughout this book, competition exists when "no single buyer or seller can influence prices and there is *perfect information*." Mediating structures are critically important as providers of information. Realistically, of course, "perfect" information is impossible to obtain, but it is possible to have good enough information, of high enough quality to make well-informed decisions.

If parents and students are expected to choose among schools, interest in the quality and character of a given school is not abstract—it has real consequences for real people.

In a choice system, how can uninformed parents choose? Obviously, they can't choose wisely or well without help.

The major thing we've learned from research into school effectiveness over the past decade is something most parents have known all along. It matters which school a student attends, and it matters a good deal. All things being equal, it makes a difference to go to a good school, rather than a second-rate one. There is nothing surprising in that statement to most Americans.

The opposite of a good school is not necessarily a bad school. It can be another kind of good school. But once again, what are parents to do when uninformed about choice or confused by it? Access to balanced, objective, and accurate information about schools is essential to a choice system. The consumer is king only if he is informed. Particularly in education, knowledge is power.

Most members of the middle class will find choice a congenial process. They will be able to inform themselves reasonably well and reasonably accurately, learning about elementary and secondary schools in the same way they learn about day care, nursery school, doctors, dentists, and churches or synagogues.

The concern about choice and good information centers— and properly so—on the low-income parent, the parent with limited education and limited access to conventional information sources. If anything, his children need a good school even more than middle-class youngsters do, but his ability to choose wisely may be severely constrained.

Albert Shanker, president of the American Federation of Teachers, says, "The poor don't have ready access to all of the available resources, and they often get ripped off in a market system." He rightly insists that parental choice systems have to include special efforts to inform minorities and the poor of options available to them.

Fortunately, there is a growing body of evidence about the best ways to provide information to parents. They include such tried and true methods as community outreach workers, parent and community meetings, school open houses, information booths in shopping centers and libraries, mailings to homes, and radio and television public service advertising. Very important, as well, are "coffees" held in private homes and community institutions, including churches, clubs, and fraternal associations.

Differences among communities must be recognized, including such obvious factors as size, location, and demographics. The needs of non-English-speaking families required bilingual outreach workers and bilingual media coverage. Sparsely populated areas should get more radio and TV coverage. Peer recruitment will be more effective at the secondary than elementary level.

Although choice systems are not yet the norm, a large number have been in place for a long enough time to provide useful information on what parents need to know and how to provide that information. The U.S. Department of Education, for example, has surveyed 37 school districts to identify strategies used to inform parents about education options, and a number of private sector education groups have prepared publications on the implementation of choice systems, with special attention to the question of informing families.

Finally, it's important to remember that a functioning choice system, once in place, establishes new relationships and new attitudes. Parents no longer have to grin and bear it. If their school is not performing adequately, they can have a heart-to-heart with the principal and teachers. The prospect of losing a dissatisfied family acts as an incentive for the school to respond. If the school does not, the family will—by choosing another school. In a choice system, the stakes are real, and parents have a strong incentive to inform themselves and act on that information.

We have discussed choice, diversity, and the introduction of market mechanisms in the public sector as the centerpiece of our reform strategy to revitalize the nation's schools. Is it possible to implement such ideas, or are they simply pipe dreams, idle musings of reformers out of touch with the reality of public education? We believe the evidence speaks for itself.

Limited choice systems are now in place in hundreds of districts across the nation, and there are more on the drawing boards. They have been used to increase racial integration, to upgrade the image of the schools, to increase public support, and to increase student and teacher morale.

They are the preferred remedy in desegregation cases today, instead of compulsory busing. In cases like Kansas City and St. Louis, magnet schools have been supported by plaintiffs' civil rights attorneys. In Massachusetts, the state director for desegregation, Charles Glenn, relies almost exclusively on choice systems to bring about successful racial integration. The Massachusetts approach is so successful in Cambridge that choice is compulsory there. While that may sound like an oxymoron, Cambridge is one of the few communities in the nation that has instituted choice in every one of its schools. (In most communities, choice is still limited to a select number of schools.)

We are witnessing, slowly and incrementally, a movement

toward what we describe as public sector markets. As we have indicated, we believe such markets are ideally suited to education, for their immediate effect is to change the locus of decision making from the bureaucrat to the family where it belongs. Families are competent to make such decisions (with or without help), and the school system is *better off* providing service to willing customers than operating like a monopoly.

One indicator of the increasing importance of choice is a special report by the nation's premier education publication, *Education Week*. The twenty-four page supplement, *The Call For Choice: Competition in the Educational Marketplace*, ran in June 1987. The analysis concluded that choice systems may "provide an effective, grass roots means for making education reform a reality." It went on to say that "choice . . . giving the parents the right to select their children's schools from among a range of possible options . . . has gained a new respectability over the past two years. . . . An assortment of bipartisan groups, from the National Governors' Association to the Carnegie Task Force on Teaching as a Profession, has recognized what was already apparent to many parents: The concept may hold vast potential for revitalizing public schools."

Schools of choice exist now in communities across the country: Rochester, N.Y., San Diego, Chicago, Miami, Albuquerque, Minneapolis, Fall River and Cambridge, Mass., and Kansas City, Mo., to name a few.

In Minneapolis, for example, more than two-thirds of the district's students attend magnet schools. The former superintendent, Richard Green, said the Minneapolis magnet system (started in 1971 with a federal government grant) has had "a tremendous impact on attitude. When parents can choose where their kids go to school, they tend to give a lot of support to that effort. There's nothing except positives that can come out of that kind of experience."

According to *Education Week*, magnet schools have turned around Buffalo, New York, once regarded as one of the worst urban districts in the state. Of New York's five largest cities, Buffalo had the highest proportion of students needing remediation in 1976. Ten years later, it had the lowest. Former Buffalo superintendent Eugene Reveille said, "There's ample evidence that [magnets] restored confidence in the schools." Not only did district test scores climb, but the dropout rate fell, and is now about the same for minority and white students.

Improvement is not restricted to Buffalo. As *Fortune* has pointed out, New York City's Spanish Harlem, which includes Community School District 4, climbed from thirty-second place out of thirty-two districts to sixteenth place in 1989. The number of students reading at grade level rose from 16 percent to 68 percent. The secret? As *Fortune* observed, "A network of elementary and junior high schools from which parents are free to choose the one they like best for their children, regardless of where they live in the district."

Fortune continued, "the market mechanism operates: Schools get better and more various by competing to offer what people want. Those that offer it successfully flourish; the others do not."

From the perspective of public schools, competition cuts in two directions. Not only do public schools compete with each other, they continue to compete with private schools. But the nature of that competition changes. As Buffalo superintendent Reveille pointed out, public magnet schools are attracting youngsters from private and parochial schools. The same refrain is echoed by superintendents with magnet schools across the country. Although the Center for Education Statistics does not collect such school change data, Richard Wallace of Pittsburgh and John Murphy, superintendent in Charlotte, N.C. (formerly superintendent in Prince George's County, Maryland), are both convinced that their enrollments have climbed by several thousand students, because of their successful magnet programs.

Murphy insists that magnet schools are a powerful lever to increase school quality. "My strategy is to use the schools of choice to bring about revolution in the school system," he says. Murphy reports that parents will wait in line as long as three days to enroll in a magnet school: "They are the same people who were saying, 'There's no way you can get me to go on a bus down to those inner-city schools,' Now they're saying, 'I'll wait in line to go there.' "

Murphy and other superintendents who have committed themselves to magnet schools see them as the wave of the future. As Murphy says, magnets "are the cutting edge of where we want to be in ten years."

Magnet schools can open other doors, as well. They encourage new kinds of cooperation between schools and other community resources in both the public and private sector. One of Buffalo's magnets is at the Buffalo Zoo. A Prince George's magnet takes advantage of the University of Maryland campus. A Houston magnet has allied itself with a major teaching hospital. A New York City magnet has special relationships with prospective employers. A downtown Philadelphia magnet has the largest Future Farmers of America chapter in the country.

Superintendent Reveille of Buffalo said that magnets "have worked to upgrade our entire system. I believe that you can't have too many choices. The more choices you have, the better the education you can offer."

Magnet supporters begin to sound more like free market entrepreneurs and less like government bureaucrats. *Education Week* quoted Faye Bryant who, as associate superintendent in charge of magnet schools in Houston said: "There is competition between magnets and neighborhood schools, and between magnets and magnets, so everyone benefits."

As knowledge and experience with choice systems become more widespread, public interest and support for choice continue to increase. The 22nd Annual Gallup Poll of the Public's Attitudes Toward the Public Schools, commissioned by the *Phi Delta Kappan* magazine, shows a gradual increase over the past decade of support for education vouchers and a gradual decline in opposition. But the numbers still cluster around the middle in response to the question about public, parochial, and private school choice: 44 percent favored vouchers in 1987 and 41 percent opposed, a shift from 43 percent in favor and 46 opposed six years earlier.

By way of contrast, when asked in 1990, "Do you favor or

oppose allowing students . . . to choose" which public schools
to attend, 62 percent favored choice, 31 percent opposed it.

In 1990, when asked if they favored choice, men and women
responded nearly identically in favor, at 61 and 63 percent, respectively. Indeed, in all categories but one—race—the numbers
are nearly constant. Age, community size, education level, income, and region produced responses only two or three percentage points apart. But 72 percent of nonwhites, and only 60 percent of whites, support choice!

The message is clear—the American public wants a free
market for education with choice and competition—they are
ready for it. They believe it will work, and that it will strengthen
the schools.

One element of choice systems demands special attention.
Are schools of choice elitist institutions that exclude the poor and
racial minorities? In light of American history, and a dual system
that was "legal" until *Brown* v. *Board of Education*, it's a fair
question.

Rather than leading to greater racial isolation, choice will
lead to less. Remember, magnet schools were originally created
to bring about voluntary racial integration, and on balance, they
have succeeded. Children of all races are content to attend school
with one another—if they like the school. Magnet schools demonstrate that the school ethos is more important than race.

Skeptics remain, however, and we concede that in some
cases their concern is legitimate. Unfettered choice in some circumstances could lead to greater racial isolation. But choice systems, unlike monopolies, lend themselves to a straightforward
solution that has been tried in the past and can be used in the
future: controlled choice. This device limits the movement of
youngsters among schools when a transfer would adversely affect a school's racial balance. Such a requirement could reasonably be imposed for the first few years of implementation to
assure racial integration.

An even more important step has not yet been tried on a
large scale—regional magnet schools as opposed to district magnet schools. They should exist in a choice system. They would
accelerate the pace of racial integration more than any other

reform we know of, because they would break the segregated housing patterns that account for today's segregated schools.

The idea has been attempted in a preliminary way in St. Louis and will be tried in Kansas City, but it deserves a test in every major city in the nation. At minimum, states should eliminate any barriers to the creation of regional magnets. States are now the senior partner in financing schools, and they could underwrite the cost of regional metropolitan magnet schools as a sign of commitment to education excellence and racial integration.

The private sector provides an important illustration of what the public sector should emulate. Gonzaga High School, a Jesuit school in downtown Washington, D.C., is a regional magnet school. It draws students from the whole metropolitan area. In fact, it numbers among its alumni graduates who commuted from Baltimore, some the sons of sleeping car porters who sought out the high quality of Gonzaga as an affordable alternative to their local public school.

Gonzaga is not only racially integrated—it is integrated by social class, including students who are the sons of senior civil servants, prominent attorneys and physicians, lobbyists and diplomats, as well as children of hourly employees and members of the working class. School and community service is a requirement for graduation.

Admittedly, Gonzaga is a special school, but it serves no good purpose to dismiss it as a private sector idiosyncrasy or as an aberration out of reach of the public sector. As a voluntary magnet school, Gonzaga can make demands on its students— and can become fully integrated—without sacrificing its goals or purposes. On the contrary, integration reinforces its goals and purposes. Ironically, the best public schools rarely have the opportunity to integrate if the neighborhoods they serve are not integrated.

Some of the nation's finest public schools—schools with a social conscience, as well as high academic standards—remain virtually lily white. Walt Whitman in Montgomery County, Maryland, Gunn in Palo Alto, California, and New Trier, north of Chicago, are institutions that would not be largely white if they were in the private sector. No self-respecting college preparatory private school would permit itself to have a student profile of the kind those exclusive public schools have.

Typically, public school educators dismiss schools like Gonzaga with the observation that "you can do it in the private sector, not the public." We want to know, why not? Why can't public schools of choice begin to look more like Gonzaga? We speak in this instance not of Gonzaga's religious character, but Gonzaga's academic, pedagogical, and moral character. A public school of choice can look like Gonzaga. It can have high standards, it can be integrated, it can perform.

Choice, then, brings us full circle to a question we touched on in the beginning of this chapter. It is so important it must be reemphasized. How would a choice system be funded, and what would the impact of the funding system be? A choice system that stresses the primacy of the customer rather than the producer must be funded on that basis. Dollars must follow students. Only when they enroll would schools earn income. That is the single most important element of a choice system, for it puts real meaning into choice. Schools must be responsive, or they lose their customers, just as business does. Money talks.

There is a corollary requirement that is equally important. If schools earn their income, then they must be free to spend it. There must be school site budgeting, not as a district accounting device, but as a true cost or profit center. Only in that way can the school enjoy the autonomy necessary to exist in a free market, for that is the logic of the business metaphor. As we will see in the next chapter, choice is not just essential to consumer satisfaction—and eventually to teacher and principal satisfaction—but it has major structural implications. If education choice is to be more than symbolic, there must be a major restructuring of the schools.

3

Restructuring: The Business of Education

We are slowly coming to realize that many of the principles and models that have guided such things as our economic development, land use, energy use and distribution, and management are anachronistic. As we come to better understand . . . . we will presumably align our practices with more appropriate theories. The same thing must occur with regard to education in the schools.

—John Goodlad
"Studies of Schooling"
Phi Delta Kappan

AMERICAN SCHOOLS, once the envy of the world, are still best suited to the economic and social needs of the early to mid-twentieth century. They bear little or no relationship to the needs of the present or the future.

The contemporary school is an outgrowth of the scientific management movement of the early twentieth century. The most important part of that movement was the belief that regimentation fostered efficient productivity. Whether the job was making steel or teaching school, raw materials would be processed in a repetitive fashion in a central place by a mass of workers supervised by a few skilled supervisors.

The theory was that if there was a science of industrial production, there was also a science of education, and it could be organized in the same manner. The teacher would be the worker manning the production line. The student would be the product. The principal would be the foreman, and the superintendent, the CEO. The school board or committee would be the corporate board of trustees, and the citizens would be the shareholders. Curriculum guides and lesson plans would be developed and approved by the central office, as would books and tests. Teachers would punch time clocks just as industrial workers did. In short, schools would be small factories of learning, with all that that implied.

Mass education had become a reality, at least in the lower grades. The system was designed to respond to the masses, pour knowledge into students, and squeeze work out of teachers, while running few, if any, risks. It was anti-intellectual and hostile to creativity, innovation, and entrepreneurship. It was an education bureaucracy, the purpose of which was to suspend the exercise of judgment. It was an education assembly line, designed to produce a perfectly uniform product by using production processes that employed the labor of people smart enough to follow the teacher's guide.

In fairness to the designers of the system, it did fit the society of the time. It was consistent with what was known about social organization and teaching. It reflected the realities of demographics and social class. But in retrospect, it was narrow, prescriptive, and limiting.

In a matter of decades, we went from an agrarian to an industrial economy, and we are now rapidly moving through the postindustrial era where the majority of the educated workforce operates not with their hands, but with their minds. We are a knowledge-based society.

Why then are we saddled with a school system organized along the lines of the factory and governed by the agricultural calendar?

If our public schools are to provide us with a modern workforce, prepared to function productively in this postindustrial knowledge-based society, then they must restructure, not only in terms of content and curriculum, but in terms of organization and performance.

Take note that restructuring is not exclusively a task for the schools. It is a challenge for every organization in a changing society. In the modern world, the most dramatic examples of restructuring are modern corporations. Indeed, only those that have restructured survive. Everybody knows the story of the buggy whip manufacturer that didn't recognize the impact of the automobile. Now, schools have the opportunity to take some powerful lessons from those savvy corporations that have learned to restructure.

Xerox Corporation has undergone a massive restructuring. The introduction in 1959 of the Xerox 914, the first plain-paper copier, launched an entire new industry and one of the greatest success stories in the history of American business. That success led to an era of feverish growth. The company's manufacturing facilities became highly labor-intensive. It built an enormous overhead structure of indirect white collar workers. Its organization became clogged with too many checks and balances. And probably most damaging of all, it became arrogant and complacent. Xerox was in the enviable position of being able to sell almost everything it made at whatever price it wanted to charge. Virtually every major company in this country at that time was in the same position.

The American corporation had begun to think that market dominance was natural, that American technology and know-how were a given, and that the rest of the world would follow in our wake. For a while, that was true. But the reality of global competition has sobered us all. We now realize that America does not have a monopoly on intelligence, organization, marketing, sales, or research and development. The one thing the American corporation has going for it is the relentless pressure of tough competitors. It holds us to high standards, and keeps us from letting our guard down.

Necessity, driven by the reality of the competitive market, forces change. What did Xerox do to regain lost market share from the Japanese and rebuild its domestic sales? It restructured. Xerox restructured to improve efficiency, output, and quality—

all within the context of finding new processes, new markets, and new ways of doing things better.

Schools now, more than ever, need to improve efficiency and quality and find new ways of doing things better. In order to do so, we believe they must restructure.

Consider what's going on now. One-fourth of the nation's young people drop out before finishing high school. Another one-fourth don't graduate with the skills necessary to find work, or they go on to postsecondary education needing remedial help. Those numbers are not new. They describe a pattern that is now several decades old. Our school system is failing about half of its students. That means it's only satisfying the needs and interests of approximately 50 percent of them. Does that suggest a school system that works? We think not.

A rejection rate that high would lead to bankruptcy in the business world. Only a monopoly could tolerate it for long, and in the business world, even a monopoly that behaved that way would be subject to consumer pressure. Our purpose here is not to point the finger of blame, but to make one simple point. Our schools are failing at least half of our students. They have done so for decades. And there is no reason to believe that business as usual, or incremental change, will make any difference.

Let us imagine what the school of the future should look like. It has two theoretical foundations and several practical applications, which we examine later in detail.

The first fundamental aspect uses the modern company as the point of reference. The modern school should look less like a factory and more like the best high-tech companies, with lean structures, flat organizations, and decision making pushed to the lowest possible level. The modern high-tech company has fewer middle managers, and those that remain act less like controllers and more like colleagues and collaborators.

Secondly, the modern school must develop standards of performance measurement to let it show the world what it does, and how it measures it. The idea of performance measurement is probably the single most important contribution that corporate America can make to the schools.

Performance measurement is discussed more fully in chapter five, *Standards*, but we mention it here because it's an important part of restructuring. Student knowledge has to be measured more sensitively and accurately. Without new measurement techniques and tools, the idea of restructuring has little or no meaning.

Without new performance standards, genuine restructuring is impossible. School structure of the past century—grouping children by age, in classrooms, seated before the teacher who lectures, gives quizzes and tests, and then assigns letter grades— made sense in a less sophisticated, less complex world when there were no better performance measures. When there was no better way to tell whether, or how much, a child profited from being in school, the old system fit.

That's why state legislatures, school committees, superintendents, and even voters still tend to measure, define, and describe schools by what goes into them: the number of books in the library, teachers on the faculty, dollars per pupil, or students in a classroom. It's easy to count the things that go into a school, but difficult to measure output or performance.

Once performance is accurately measured, schools will have a proxy for efficiency and effectiveness. It will no longer be necessary to regulate schools and ensnare them in skeins of red tape. It should be of no concern to a state legislature how a school meets its academic objectives. What's important is that it does.

Such measurement techniques are well within our grasp. They are already well defined in the case of second language mastery. The U.S. State Department Foreign Language Institute, for example, has developed a widely accepted system of testing and certifying students. The tests use multiple choice and true and false answers, but they also include written essays and analysis of written material. They measure verbal skills (including oral as well as written examinations).

Performance measures do more than just document individual accomplishment. They provide indicators for organizational effectiveness and efficiency, precisely the kinds of measures that business must live with. The modern company is not bureaucratic and prescriptive precisely because it has performance measures at its disposal. The CEO doesn't worry about detailed rules and regulations for managers and scientists. He knows he can count on them to do the best they can, because their performance is being accurately measured.

Analysts argue that measuring the effectiveness of business is relatively easy, compared with measuring the effectiveness of a school. After all, business has profit—its bottom line. But if it's hard to measure what schools do, then we have to work harder at the task. That it is hard does not suggest that we abandon the enterprise. We must redouble our efforts to solve the problem.

We have developed some practical restructuring proposals that we are convinced will prepare schools—and their teachers and students—for the twenty-first century. If choice is to become a part of the school system of tomorrow, if competition within the public sector is to become the norm, if schools and teachers are to be held accountable, then the restructuring we propose must have definite limits, purpose, and shape.

Every public school district with more than 2,500 students should reorganize into a year-round magnet system. We suggest a cutoff point, because of what economists call "natural monopoly." In other words, if a school district is too small, there aren't going to be enough schools in that district to compete with one another. We would, however, expect to see some competition between small districts, even if there is only limited competition within them.

A magnet school is an open enrollment school organized around an academic or vocational specialty that attracts both youngsters and teachers because of its distinctive educational personality. Magnet schools were first devised to achieve voluntary racial integration. The idea was to make the schools attractive enough so that involuntary busing would become voluntary. Some of the nation's most distinguished and well-known public schools are magnet schools: Bronx Science, Brooklyn Tech, Boston Latin, Lowell in San Francisco, Aviation in Queens, Performing Arts in Manhattan. These are schools that enjoy national reputations because of their high levels of accomplishment in areas of specific instruction.

Magnet schools are special centers of competence. In our plan they would become the norm. There would be high schools specializing in the humanities, math, science, skilled vocational areas, languages, and the arts. There would be lower schools organized around unique learning methods and teaching styles.

They would be open year round, which is to say they would be open for learning and instruction continuously throughout the year. We don't mean 180 days of instruction distributed across the full calendar year. That's the way most year-round schools are currently organized. Some children attend school in the fall, winter, and spring with summer vacations. Others attend school in the summer and take a vacation in the fall, winter, or spring. Year-round schools of that type are not designed for year-round learning. They are a device to get greater utilization of the physical plant.

We believe that year-round schools should meet day in and day out, year round, permitting students to attend for as many days as they need to gain academic skills. For some children, that will be a 240-day school year. For others, it will mean 220 or 200 days. And for some, it might still mean 180 days, with part of the year spent in useful work, travel, or self-directed study.

This is not an idle pipe dream. There are precedents, both historical and contemporary. In the days of mass immigration to this country, it was not uncommon for some school districts to have ten-month school years for immigrants, and nine-month school years for regular students. In many of our big cities, until well after World War II, summer school was a regular part of the school year, providing opportunities for acceleration and remediation.

The secret of a successful year-round program is that it addresses the realities of modern life. Single-parent households and dual-income families need year-round schooling as a way to keep their children safe, as well as educated. In some households, parents will want the schools open on precisely the same days they work. That would mean *no* regularly scheduled school vacations, only bank holidays such as Christmas, New Year's Day, and Thanksgiving.

We should reemphasize that some magnet schools already exist in the public education system. However, year-round schools, as we define them, do not. But, in our plan, year-round schools and magnet schools are inextricably intertwined. As we have already stated, schools must reflect the larger social, economic, and cultural realities of the society in which they operate. Today's schools once did. They no longer do. Tomorrow's schools must, or they will fail.

We have already touched on the knowledge-based service economy, which changes both the nature and focus of work. Equally important, however, is the transformation of the American family. Today, 60 percent of women with children over the age of three work outside the home, and every sign indicates that this trend will become even more pronounced. Even more women will work outside the home, for longer hours and longer careers, and this will have profound implications for both society at large and the schools.

That means that one of the oldest and most important functions of the school—as the site of custodial care and provider of day care—must be re-examined. Today the reality for too many families is latch-key children, youngsters who return to an empty home after school. We are convinced that this social strategy courts disaster. No society can afford to leave its children without adult supervision for extended periods of time.

Year-round schools with day care are a necessary complement to the realities of the modern workforce. Parents and students need them—not all parents and not all students—but for those who do, the need is acute. Ironically, year-round schools have been a controversial reform measure, drawing strong negative reactions in many communities. In resort areas, for example, there is resistance to having year-round schools for fear of losing teen-age employees. In middle-class and professional areas, there is a fear that year-round schools will disrupt conventional vacation schedules. Among the inner-city poor—ethnic minorities in Los Angeles, for example—there is the concern that year-round schools are a device used by the power structure to take advantage of the powerless.

Those reactions are disappointing. Change of any kind is dislocating, and it tends to make any beneficiaries suspicious, particularly if they're not part of the process that leads to change. They feel that change is forced upon them, and that they are losers, not winners. But we now know enough about year-round schools to design them with the future in mind. Remember, just as the system now in place was deliberately designed to accommodate the economic realities of the nineteenth century, when children were needed for the cycle of planting and harvest, the elements of year-round schools for the future should be similarly designed to accommodate the realities of the twenty-first century.

That would mean a calendar that provides maximum coordination between work and school. It does parents little good to have to deal with a group of small vacations in lieu of one large one. Thus, the year-round calendar should be designed to provide full-time coverage, five days a week, twelve hours a day.

The year-round aspect should be voluntary, with incentives built in to increase utilization. Children who wish to go to school twelve months a year could do so. Those who prefer a traditional two-semester or three-quarter year with a long vacation could also do so. For families worried about disrupting vacation schedules, because their children are enrolled in competing semesters or quarters, there should be some guarantee that that would not happen—at least not very often.

The year-round calendar would provide added flexibility. In today's economy, some students have to work to help support their families. A system of school quarters would mean students could attend school all year long, take a quarter or two off, or combine work with school. Year-round schools also promise to even out the youth job market, particularly since enrollments would be evenly distributed throughout the year. Year-round schools would eliminate the annual June flood of young people into the workplace. They could afford to be selective and enter the job market when they think the time is best for them.

Flexible terms, a concept we discuss fully in chapter five, *Standards*, would let students complete their education at their own pace, finishing the work required at one level before moving on to the next. They would advance quickly in subjects they're good at, and more slowly in subjects that are harder for them. They would have the option of breaking out of the lock-step of the grade structure, which would be eliminated. For many students, the year-round magnet format would permit remedial work where necessary, and specialization for students with strongly developed interests, such as computers, math, or dance.

Just as students should enjoy the flexibility of choosing which semesters or quarters to attend, so, too, should teachers. Any teacher who wishes could remain on a 180-day calendar. Those who want to work full time, either year after year or only occasionally, could do so. They would then receive a 33 percent increase in salary. For example, a salary of $24,000 would rise to $32,000 a year, and a salary of $48,000 would go to $64,000 a year—but the existing salary schedule would not change.

One of the most important aspects of that part of year-round schools is that it would put teeth into the debate about teacher compensation. Full-time teachers would get full-time pay. Those who work nine months or less would get paid proportionally less.

Year-round schools will address only part of the latch-key child problem. To solve it completely, schools would have to extend the school day, offer enriched day care, and advance the age of initial enrollment to accommodate children who are now treated as pre-schoolers. The year-round program should be voluntary, not compulsory. Offer working mothers the option of year-round schools for their children, together with extended day care, and interest in year-round schools will increase substantially.

Finally, there is one element of year-round schools that is particularly important from a business perspective. Letting the physical plant and the highly trained employees of a $220-billion-a-year industry sit idle for three out of twelve months makes no sense. As Lamar Alexander said when he was governor of Tennessee, "We're not rich enough to afford that." No business could run that way, and it's clear that education can't either.

If schools are as important as we believe they are, and our economy can't flourish without them, how can we let those resources languish, underused? Business leaders are quick to point out that the competition doesn't behave that way. While the typical American student attends school 180 days a year, his Japanese counterpart—and competitor—goes to school 240 days a year. When the Japanese student graduates from high school, he or she has completed the equivalent of at least two years of a good American college.

The year-round school is the school of the future—there is no other choice if America is to meet the challenges of changing life-styles at home and the challenges of a competitive world economy abroad.

Magnet schools are just as important to the future of education. Indeed, they are essential. It should now be clear to most Americans that just as there are different people, there are different teaching and learning styles. The old idea of one best system of education is now thoroughly discredited. What we need in the future is a school system as varied as the interests, talents, and capacities of our teachers and students. We need academic schools, military schools, boarding schools, and schools for music and art, mathematics and science, technology and office skills, dance and theater. There is no reason to package all education in the same way, or treat all students and teachers as if they were identical. They're not.

Magnet schools were heralded in a *Washington Post* headline in the late 1980s: "Montgomery Magnet Schools Achieve More Than Racial Balance." Montgomery County, Maryland is one of the nation's premier public school systems, with a national reputation for excellence. The county schools and the residents have a reputation for caring about issues of equity and social justice, as well as academic excellence.

A three-year study by Montgomery County found that students from the county's racially mixed magnet schools "outperformed their peers at other schools in reading and math by the end of the sixth grade." On standardized reading tests, sixth graders of all races in the county's fourteen magnet schools scored 10 percent higher than students at similar, non-magnet elementary schools; math scores were 18 percent higher. While the researchers would only speculate about the reasons, they emphasized features such as "special curriculum" and "positive climate." They were hopeful "that the findings may signal the beginning of a trend of academic excellence resulting in part from the learning climate . . . in magnet schools."

Not surprisingly, children who transfer into magnet schools tend to enjoy school more and are more likely to form interracial friendships. Equally important, parents of magnet school students tend to do more school volunteer work.

In fact, researchers in the Montgomery County study also found that magnet schools went "beyond test scores" to a "high degree of student satisfaction and parent involvement at the magnet schools." Equally important, teacher expectations about student performance in the magnet schools were relatively "unclouded by race," a commentary on the fact that teachers frequently expect less of minority youngsters, more of middle-class white youngsters.

Restructuring so that magnet schools become the norm gives choice systems meaning and impact. Schools that attract and hold students succeed. Schools that do not change or fold.

Restructuring should bring about one more practical change. To use our business metaphor, school district offices should become service centers—helping schools, instead of dictating to them. Schools should be managed by their principals and teachers. They should design their own curriculums, set their own specialties, and compete with other schools in a new education marketplace fueled by diversity and free choice. Suppliers— schools and their teachers and administrators—should be free to organize themselves as they wish, subject to a simple market test.

The central headquarters as service center is a novel idea in a school context, but not in the business world. Genuine professionals, to do their jobs well, must be given autonomy. And if schools of choice become a reality, so too must school site budgeting. The principal and staff must be responsible for as many decisions as possible at the building level. That will mean tough trade-offs between administrative overhead and teaching staff. And it will mean deciding whether to put limited resources into teacher salaries or materials.

Visualize a grade school with ninety or so seven- and eight-year-olds, ordinarily thought of as three third grades. If the building principal and staff are professionals, they should be the ones who decide the staffing configuration for that group of children. Three fully licensed teachers, one for each group? One master teacher and two teacher trainees? Two senior teachers and three aides? There is no correct answer. The principal and staff should decide based on the specifics of their own situation.

If the building is the proper location for decision making, then the office of the superintendent should be a service center, not a command post barking orders. The building principal must be in a position to "buy" or not "buy" the services the superintendent proposes to offer. Curriculum coordination, psychological services, counseling, area or regional coordination, textbook acquisition, library services, itinerant special education services, and the like should be made available by the central office and purchased on an as-needed basis by schools. If the schools neither want nor need certain services, they will have resources to secure those they do need, and the superintendent will have to offer new services or reconfigure.

Without such market discipline within the system, bureaucracies become ever more hidebound and unresponsive. Indeed, bureaucrats without the pressure of supply and demand become autocrats attempting to perform activities for which there is no demand. In Xerox, there are two kinds of customers—external and internal. We all know who the external customers are. The task in the modern company or school is to identify the internal customers, understand their requirements, and meet them. If there are no requirements to understand and meet, the functions those internal customers represent are likely candidates for abolishment. At least, they should be. We describe the concept more fully in chapter five.

We have discussed the restructuring of schools, but it's important to realize that they can't be restructured in isolation. Teaching must be rethought and reorganized as well. The two must fit, hand in glove. New teaching responsibilities and opportunities require new organizational arrangements.

In the restructured school of the future, the teacher will be part of the team, a professional who participates in decision making, not a cog in a bureaucratic wheel. So, if teachers are part of a team that decides about hiring and firing, for example, they will need to develop new relationships with each other and deepen their understanding of what their new responsibilities entail.

In the next chapter we discuss teacher professionalism in

detail. However, we mention teachers here because the process of teaching needs restructuring, as well as the schools themselves. Teachers should be expected to make curriculum textbook decisions in the reconfigured school of the future, in just the way college and university professors do today. For example, when state graduation requirements call for mastery of a second language to a demonstrated level of proficiency, language teachers should be free to identify the approach, the methods, and the textbooks they will use to bring their students along. Who knows better?

A final issue in restructuring is the use of technology. We have gone from the age of the ditto machine to the age of the lap-top computer. Yet, technology has had virtually no impact on today's schools. We believe it can drive the school of the future— but only if the schools of today organize for it. You cannot parachute technology into an organization and expect it just to settle in. To use technology intelligently, you have to organize for it. Computers, for example, have been of marginal help to the schools, because schools were not organized to use them. Technologies in and of themselves are simply curiosities. They must fit the organization, and the organization must fit the technology. It is the lack of fit that has produced such limited results in the uses of education technology. Most schools, as they are presently organized, are not in a position to use technology intelligently.

Paul Strassmann, a former Xerox vice-president and a recognized expert on information systems, testified before a congressional technology task force recently. He made two important points. First, technology has the best potential for improving productivity. Second, companies most likely to benefit from technology are those that have streamlined their management, focused on quality, and found innovative ways to add value for their customers.

In other words, companies that have organized for technology get the most out of it. Xerox, for example, cut production costs by more than 50 percent and reduced the time for getting new machines to market by as much as 30 percent since 1982. Xerox also cut the cost of new copiers to half that of the models they replaced. Xerox didn't do that just with better technology, but by changing the way it does its work. Xerox did it by delegating decision-making power down through a much more decentralized organization.

If schools restructure to use technology and learning theories effectively, we won't need to spend billions of dollars on new school buildings or worry that classes are too big. In the school of the future, classes will probably be bigger than they are now, with a combination of team teaching and computers, with an emphasis on collaborative learning—learning by doing and peer tutoring. One student coaches and teaches another. The student tutor is usually, but not always, older, and he is more academically advanced. The effect of student tutoring is that both the tutor and his student learn from each other.

These approaches require schools to be organized differently, and teachers and principals to behave differently. The issue here is not to hold teachers' and administrators' feet to the fire, although that's part of it. The issue is to provide educators, students, and the taxpaying public with some assurance that education is worthwhile—that it does what it says it will do. Make no mistake about it. The American public will not give education a blank check, particularly in light of the fierce competition for limited resources.

We are convinced that restructuring is an imperative that cannot be ignored. It will be painful and difficult, and one of its principal outcomes will be to put the public schools into a competitive market where they must perform, change, or fold. Performance measures are a critically important part of the scenario. They will make it possible for students and their families to choose among schools, and for taxpayers and their elected representatives to be informed about education, what it costs, and what benefits it brings. We propose restructuring, not as an end in itself, but as a way to achieve a larger and more important set of goals—education excellence and accountability.

In the existing system, schools get a free ride—the good, the bad, and the indifferent are treated equally. That's a formula for failure and decreasing public confidence.

4

Professionalism and the Modern Teacher

A teacher affects eternity; he can never tell where his influence stops.
—Henry Brooks Adams

A RESTRUCTURED SCHOOL SYSTEM that gives teachers choice and autonomy won't work unless teachers are true professionals—masters of an academic knowledge base, and prepared for the autonomy, variety, and entrepreneurship of the school of the future. Teaching today is blue collar work, even though it's fashionable to describe teaching as a profession. In only a very few schools can teaching be truly described as a profession. That's not to say that there aren't large numbers of teachers who are professionals—many are. Indeed, the wonder is that there are so many professionals when most schools are organized to discourage, even disparage, them.

Meeting superb teachers—teachers of the year, for example—we are struck with just how good they are. They're smart, dedicated, hard-working individuals. They have high morale, they love their work, they don't regret having gone into teaching. They would do it again. They're an inspiration to their students and colleagues.

They share one other trait, however, not widely talked about in large school districts or schools of education—they are "canny outlaws," system beaters, creative and responsible rule benders. They have to be to succeed, because in most school districts—especially the large ones—the deck is stacked against the creative, imaginative, and entrepreneurial teacher.

As we stated earlier, most of our schools look a lot like factories, and almost without exception, have the gray personality of a government bureaucracy. Working conditions are uniform—uniformly drab and difficult. Salaries are on a fixed schedule that bears little or no relationship to accomplishment. Internal and external incentives and rewards are few and far between. There is little opportunity for true collegiality and disciplinary development, as there is in colleges, universities, and private R & D settings. The physical plant is frequently inadequate to the task expected of the teacher.

Rare is the teacher with his own office, or even a regular place to work away from students, or to make or receive a phone call in private. Professionals in other walks of life would find that incomprehensible and unacceptable. Examine another aspect of schools under which teachers in most of our big cities labor. The custodians control the buildings. Literally. They have the keys to the building, the keys to the rooms, and they control heating and lighting. Teachers who want to come early or stay late cannot do so because they are denied access to the building and their classrooms. The teacher who proposes to engage in an extracurricular activity must get permission, just as the student must. Imagine professionals who have to punch time clocks—many teachers do.

But the most telling way in which teachers differ from other professionals is how they are supervised. Typically, teachers report to administrators. Compare that with doctors and lawyers. Administrators report to them. Most hospitals, for example, will not waste a trained physician in a senior management position. Hospital administrators are typically not doctors, they're trained administrative personnel who report to the physicians. In the same way, law firms have management committees made up of senior partners, but they don't oversee day-to-day operations—they hire an administrator who reports to them.

This is not a trivial distinction, nor are the differences semantic. The hard fact is that teachers are not treated like professionals, and the ones who are professionals have become professionals in spite of the system, not because of it. Some might argue that it's all a name game. The real professionals are the administrators with teachers as their agents. Or the real professional is the superintendent, with the teachers *and* the administrators as his agents. Perhaps that model was once true, perhaps it even made sense.

Indeed, it was the model for most of American industry and it worked reasonably well in that setting until sometime after World War II. But that was the nature of the production process and the product that was its object. Specific skills were not needed to produce a unique product. That was the triumph of the assembly line. Artisans and craftsmen were no longer needed. So too in the schools.

But if we have learned anything about education over the millennia, we know that the secret of success lies in the interaction between the teacher and the student. If you doubt that, think back to your own experience in school and remember the teachers who influenced you. You'll remember several teachers of distinction, men and women who changed your life, because of their devotion to their calling, their high standards, and their determination to share their insights with their students. That's the meaning of the old saying, "good teaching never ends."

It's worth examining here what teacher professionalism should be. First of all, professionalism is not simply changing names or titles to improve the image of teaching. It has to be a genuine statement about qualifications and performance, or it's not worth undertaking. The first task is to define the term. A professional is someone who *professes*, someone who commands a special body of knowledge that only he and his fellow professionals possess. It's a body of knowledge that sets him apart from the run of the mill. It's knowledge acquired through study and practice. It's knowledge of interest to those who don't have it as well as those who do. Thus, the professional is in demand. There are clients, customers, patients, parishioners, students, disciples, all of whom desire to benefit from what the professional knows.

A professional, in addition to commanding a body of specialized knowledge, is a member of a group, a *profession*, an association of colleagues who also command the same body of knowledge, often in different degrees of accomplishment, depending on the length and depth of their scholarship or participation in their work.

Perhaps most important, a professional enters into relationships voluntarily—compulsion and professionalism are incompatible. The professional freely accepts or rejects clients or students, just as a professional's clients freely engage or disengage with the professional. The professional, by accepting membership in a profession, also assumes special obligations and duties. He must be faithful to the canons of the profession, he must honor his commitment to his client, he can't break the link—even if the going gets tough, and he must respect the integrity and privacy of his client. It is a special and privileged relationship.

What is it that the professional does that creates this special relationship, and what is the nature of the professional's knowledge that permits it in the first place? The professional is expected to take his body of special knowledge and apply it to the special circumstances of his client, customer, or student. In a word, the professional is expected to exercise informed judgment. It is the antithesis of bureaucracy.

Imagine a high-tech company attempting to look to the future, identifying pioneering technologies and envisioning possibilities, without relying on independent and autonomous professionals.

Autonomy, mastery, and independence, then, are the hallmarks of the professional. We see that most vividly in the learned professions—lawyers, doctors, scientists, professors in colleges and universities. Is that so much pie in the sky for elementary and secondary education? Does real professionalism have a place there? We are convinced that it does, that it must. Without it, our schools will founder, because they can no longer be run on the bureaucratic models of the past.

We believe that the first step in increasing professionalism in our schools is to provide more professional running room for teachers, to let those who are good get out from under the heavy hand of rule and regulation. The ideas we have discussed in preceding chapters will create the environment for professionalism to flourish—choice and magnet schools, for example, will provide significant opportunity for teachers ready to seize the moment. But creating an environment conducive to professionalism is not all that needs to be done.

Not all teachers are ready to act like professionals, in large measure because they have not been prepared to accept such responsibility. Most teachers are not being trained to be professionals. We must, then, go back to the beginning, to teacher training. As most readers already know, it's a dismal business, often excruciatingly boring, often irrelevant. That's its reputation, among teachers and non-teachers alike.

What might be done to improve teacher education, both its reputation and its effectiveness? The single most important thing would be to bring it into line with the preparation of other professionals.

First-class professional training throughout the world has two elements: deep grounding in the content of the discipline—knowledge of law, or medicine, or architecture, for example; and hands-on experience and practice under the direct guidance of a master—the medical internship and residency is the model most appropriate to teaching. The experienced and seasoned practitioner who has seen it all schools the solidly educated but inexperienced novice. The role of the master is both to impart information and to communicate a style—a way of approaching problems, a way of thinking about issues.

Unlike law, where issues are frequently adversarial, or architecture, where the challenge is design *de novo*, in medicine the issue is first diagnostic, then prescriptive. The problem is to make or keep someone well. It is therapeutic, and in practicing his calling, the doctor is as much artist as scientist. He relies on informed judgment, as well as incontrovertible evidence.

Indeed, the doctor's real skill is his ability to make informed judgments.

The parallel in education is new licensing standards for teachers at the state level, but it will be important to remember that new standards should be flexible and diverse, not rigid and one-dimensional. In periods of reform, it is all too easy to imagine that the response to low standards is simply to jack up the old ones. Not so. In teaching, in particular, we know that there are truly "different strokes for different folks." What may be a perfectly reasonable set of standards in one setting may not work at all in another.

We have called for some significant measure of deregulation of schools, permitting those that meet their objectives to escape the regulatory reach of the state. Teacher licensing, in particular, should be an example of the deregulatory mode. There was a time when teacher licensing was a device to protect the public from the unfit. A license is, after all, permission to do something that is otherwise prohibited. Over time, however, the license to teach has become as much a barrier as a safety device, keeping out as many good people as unsatisfactory candidates.

The answer is a flexible licensing system, based in large measure on performance standards for teachers. How can what teachers *do* be measured? Knowledge of subject matter can be measured, at least with a degree of precision consistent with the needs of licensing. Teachers can be expected to pass an examination in the subject they propose to teach, just as lawyers must pass a bar exam. While it's true that mere knowledge of subject matter is no guarantee that a teacher will be good, ignorance of the subject guarantees that the teacher will not be good. A candidate for teaching, then, should be expected to demonstrate that he knows the subject he proposes to teach, and the most reasonable way to prove this assertion is to submit to a test. Together with the requirement that the prospective teacher hold a bachelor's degree from an accredited institution, a teacher examination provides some reasonable assurance of breadth and depth.

What should be tested and who should design and administer the teacher test? Teachers themselves should play a major role in designing the tests and determining what content areas should be covered, but the test selection panel should not be limited to the grade level and subject area to be examined. College and university professors in the same discipline should be included, as well as public interest members who will ensure that the test selection panel is truly representative of the discipline. Of necessity, the test must be administered by the state or at its behest, because licensing is a part of the police power of the state. But the state can and should respect the integrity of the emerging profession of teaching.

What of teaching ability, however? How should that be measured?

There's only one way to measure teaching ability, in the same setting in which it's acquired: in the lion's den. Teaching ability is acquired and demonstrated by performance as a teacher. An applicant for a license who is already a seasoned teacher from another state or county can demonstrate his command of his craft by exhibition or performance.

The novice teacher, however, has much to learn, and only one place to learn it—at the feet of a master teacher. To be sure, the current manner of student teaching is better than going into a classroom with no experience whatsoever. But unfortunately, it is the rare teacher who has the good luck to have a truly effective and structured apprenticeship. Ask any teacher where he learned to teach, and the answer will be the same: in the classroom. But too often, teaching is learned in the school of hard knocks, sink or swim. (The only other calling with less relevant preparation is parenthood.)

The education degree should be eliminated. Teachers should earn a bachelor's degree in a subject—not education—then take a fifth-year internship in a school building, under the supervision of a master teacher. The master teacher could—and should—have a joint appointment with a college or university, and the teacher-intern should continue an academic course of study to supplement the hands-on experience.

How might such a program be financed? The question is a proper one, given the realities of the budget crunch the nation faces. First, we must remember that the teacher-intern is doing socially useful work, not as much or as high quality work as the licensed teacher. But the intern is not just learning—he's contributing, as well. The most obvious solution, then, is to pay interns. Pay them less than licensed first-year teachers—how much less depends on the master teacher's supervision ratio. If one master teacher supervises six interns, for example, paying each intern only five-sixths of a full starting salary would leave one full salary—six-sixths—available to offset the cost of supervision. The equivalent of one starting salary—taken from each of the interns' salaries—would supplement the master teacher's regular salary.

Note that this arrangement puts the most significant part of teacher training in the school building where it belongs. It takes it out of the teachers' college realm of theory and speculation and makes it real, just as the medical internship does. It also means that school districts with well-developed internships can control content and attract the most promising prospective teachers. Finally, the experience of the internship itself provides a natural setting to measure teaching ability and reinforce and nurture talent.

If that approach will increase professionalism at entry level for new teachers, what is required for mature senior teachers? First, there must be the transformation of working conditions and supervisorial relationships we have already described. Teachers must play an active role in the design, selection, and implementation of the tests used to license the profession.

Teachers must also begin to play an active and decisive role in the selection of the curriculum materials and textbooks used in the classroom. They must begin to select the tests they administer to students, and they must play a more active role in the intellectual disciplines they teach, including such things as release time for study and professional development.

Choice, magnet schools, transferring of responsibility to the building level, school site budgeting, treating administrative offices as service centers rather than command-control headquarters—all of those changes will make a very real difference in the professional lives of the teachers.

But having done all those things, one major change remains: Teacher compensation must be designed around a professional framework. Today, teachers in most jurisdictions are paid for longevity and the number of credit hours earned after the bachelor's degree. That scheme may have made sense once upon a time. Using the factory metaphor again, paying teachers on the basis of longevity was in some sense fair. If all schools were the same, and all teaching assignments basically identical and interchangeable (except for the specific knowledge component— chemistry, rather than Spanish, for example), it made sense to pay long-timers more than short-timers. A reward for sticking it out also acted as an incentive to begin, and it was consistent with compensation packages in industry, though not with the compensation packages of professionals.

Paying teachers more for additional hours of study after the bachelor's degree made primitive sense, as well. Additional hours were a proxy for additional knowledge, which, in turn, was a proxy for additional competence. In some sense, then, additional pay for additional college study was a sort of merit pay anyone could aspire to, and no one would be denied. If you didn't have it, it was because you failed to earn it.

But if those two ideas once made sense, they don't any longer. Pay for longevity and pay for additional credit hours, the two steps of the conventional school salary schedule, should be replaced with pay for performance and pay for scarcity.

Pay for performance has two dimensions, one of which is non-controversial, the other of which is. People who work more and harder, all other things being equal, should get paid more. A teacher who teaches an extra class each semester, or an extra semester each year, should get paid more than the teacher who does not. That is hardly controversial. What is controversial is the idea that the teacher who teaches "better" should get paid more.

Merit pay is an idea that is not controversial in business or other professions. To the contrary, its absence would be controversial. In the real world of the private sector, we are convinced that pay and performance must be linked. To fail to do so is profoundly demoralizing. The high achiever is penalized, and the underachiever is unfairly rewarded. Neither person profits, because unfair and inadequate reward systems are self-defeating. It's an old saw in teaching that it is at once the highest and lowest paid of the professions, because the worst are paid what the best are, and the best are paid what the worst are.

We recognize that teaching is a collaborative, cooperative, and collegial undertaking, that its norms are not competitive, and that its history does not include pay for performance. We further recognize that it will be difficult to introduce pay for performance into the profession. Right up front, one big problem is that giving good teachers more money still leaves bad teachers in place. Still, we believe that teaching will never be a true profession until pay for performance becomes a part of it. Indeed, we don't even think it's necessary to develop here a pay for performance plan—that's properly the responsibility of the profession. But one has to be developed if the profession is to mature.

The task is not insurmountable. In many colleges and universities, salary differentials exist on the basis of performance. Not all professors are paid the same, and however difficult the decision-making process may be, once the process is put in place, teachers live with it comfortably.

But we are prepared to offer this recommendation on one aspect of teacher compensation: Pay scarce disciplines more. Use a market test in paying teachers. Are chemistry teachers or math teachers in short supply? Pay them more. That's how the market for personnel works in the private sector, and that's how we can be assured of a long-term supply of trained people. Indeed, the failure to pay teachers on the basis of market conditions is what causes so-called teacher shortages from time to time.

In a mature economy of the kind we enjoy, short of war or plague, there are no real manpower shortages. There may be temporary supply-demand imbalances, but no fundamental personnel shortages. There may be a shortage of energy or enthusiasm by school boards when budget time for teachers' salaries rolls around. There may be a shortage of generosity—or perspicacity—by taxpayers when it comes time to pay teachers. Or there may be a shortage of adults willing to work for low pay and poor working conditions when teachers' jobs are advertised. But there is no such thing as a teacher shortage in a market economy. Shortages occur in planned economies, because compulsion doesn't work. In teaching, so-called shortages are the result of the interaction effects between licensing requirements, pay scales, and working conditions—psychic income.

Take the case of science teachers. They're in short supply, not because we failed to produce enough, but because the jobs don't appeal to them. Salaries are low, working conditions are unattractive, and the atmosphere is bureaucratic. Imagine asking a person well trained in science to forgo a well-equipped corporate lab, higher pay, exciting work, and interesting colleagues to teach science in the inner city where the building is filthy and unsafe, the students are poorly prepared and unmotivated, and the lab—if it exists at all—is in shambles with little or no equipment. To make matters worse, this teacher would become part of an impenetrable bureaucracy and be paid less than two-thirds of what he would earn in the private sector. Is it any wonder that it's hard to attract science teachers in such a setting?

But examine one magnet school, the North Carolina School of Science and Mathematics. It has well-equipped labs, the students are well prepared and highly motivated (because they're pursuing their chosen subjects), the buildings are clean and well maintained, and there is a sense of collegiality and fellowship among the faculty. Performance is rewarded, if not financially, at least psychologically, because the principal, parents, and students think highly of the science teachers. There is no shortage here. That was once true of the Bronx School of Science, but it may be true no longer. In early 1988, the *New York Times* reported that 300 school windows were broken. Only half had been reglazed because of a dispute with custodians.

There is yet another issue of teacher professionalism we must not ignore—teachers' unions. They represent a major force in the life of the public school, as well as the teacher. In fact, teaching is one of this country's most highly unionized professions. Although the two biggest unions, the National Education Association and the American Federation of Teachers, were founded in the late nineteenth century and early twentieth century respectively, they did not gain national prominence until the 1960s when teacher activism reached new heights. To many outside the schools, modern teachers' unions appear to be part of the problem. We are convinced they are part of the solution.

Teachers, particularly those in large bureaucratic systems, will need representation to help them restructure their profession.

The truth is that neither labor nor management is right all the time. Labor negotiations are to economic activity what debate is to democracy. The competition of ideas keeps both sides honest and keeps the nation as a whole strong. However, just as labor and management have common interests, they also have differences, and those differences are properly aired in the collective bargaining process. As long as labor and management bring their differences to the bargaining table and hammer them out honestly and fairly, unions are an asset, not a liability.

It would be patronizing in the extreme to suppose that management is so far-sighted and enlightened that it will always have the interest of the workers at heart. But workers deserve a voice, and this is nowhere more true than in education. As we have argued, increasing professionalism for teachers is essential in the restructured school of the future, and one of the major avenues to increased professionalism will be enlightened union leadership. As such leadership confronts the realities of the modern school and economy, it will almost certainly transform unions themselves.

It would be presumptuous for us to suggest what tomorrow's unions will look like, except to note that as schools restructure, so too must management and labor. Teachers' unions are the biggest single institutional stakeholder in public education. They have the most to gain or lose in the success or failure of the future school, and we are confident that they will help lead the way. What will be particularly interesting in the schools of the future—at least the way we envision them—is who will be management, and who will be labor?

If you want to see one version of the future, look to Xerox's old home town, Rochester, New York. There the teachers' union president, Adam Urbanski, and the superintendent, Peter McWalters, negotiated in 1987 a contract that can only be described as remarkable. Indeed, it may have been the most important collective bargaining agreement in the country since World War II. It established four levels of teaching, and created a top salary of $70,000 per year. Most important, it explicitly recognized the virtues of decentralization, magnet schools, diversity, and competition. Urbanski, who is also vice-president of the American Federation of Teachers, observed:

> The notion of giving parents a choice of public schools is predicated on two pillars of the American system: equal opportunity and open-market competition. Schools that have to compete for students are less likely to become complacent and are more apt to adjust and improve what they have to offer. Not surprisingly, schools that don't have to compete exhibit many of the characteristics of monopolies.
>
> Lack of choice limits the ability of parents and students to affect the school, heightens their sense of frustration and often leads to resignation and apathy. This cycle can and should be broken.

Increasing salaries to such a high level and increasing teacher professionalism have a price: higher student performance. The public must be assured that increased professionalism will increase performance. We are convinced that the changes we have sketched in will do just that—increase professionalism and increase performance. But if teachers are going to be held accountable for student performance, they must not be locked out of the decision-making process. (In 1991 the bloom is off the rose in Rochester. Student performance is stagnant, and New York's fiscal crisis places the school reform of 1987 at risk.)

Teacher accountability is a major concern and an objective of the Carnegie Forum's National Board for Professional Teaching Standards. The chair is former North Carolina governor James B. Hunt, Jr., and the president is James A. Kelly. The membership includes Albert Shanker of the American Federation of Teachers; Mary Futrell, former president of the National Education Association; former New Jersey governor Thomas M. Kean; and, until recently David T. Kearns, coauthor of this book. Indeed, the full list of sixty board members is a who's who of American educational and civic life. Its purpose is to do for teaching what medical specialty boards have done for medicine. Operating exclusively in the private sector—in *addition to*, not *instead of*, state licensing—medical specialty boards establish the criteria for board certification, awarded to those who are able to pass the rigorous standards imposed by the board.

The various medical certification boards are composed almost exclusively of doctors who are themselves specialists in the field and who are board certified. The purpose of these boards is to demonstrate that the profession is prepared to rise above the minimums established by the state for licensing, to establish standards that are harder to meet and will confer greater distinction on the practitioner.

If board certification is brought to a successful conclusion for teachers, it will be the single most important reform of the decade, for it will mean that teaching has come of age. Teaching will emerge from the shadows of blue collar work to become a true profession. In addition to higher status, higher pay will follow board-certified teachers, who will be a beacon to their colleagues. Indeed, the straightforward expedient of board certification would make it possible finally to give realistic structure to the salary schedule of teaching across the nation.

There is yet another parallel between modern companies and schools that is little noted and deserves attention. The sales force of any company is its principal contact with the outside world, with customers both actual and prospective. How a company relates to its customers is critical to the company's success. The best product will not sell itself, any more than an inferior product can be sold by even the most gifted salesperson. There is, then, a symbiosis that must be maintained between sales, design, manufacturing, marketing, and production.

Can sales forces offer the schools any lessons? We believe they can. First, the salesperson, to be effective, must know the product line backward and forward. So, too, must the teacher. More important, the salesperson must know his customer's needs. That means understanding the client's business, as well as the client. A salesperson must be knowledgeable and not just personable. He can't sell a product he doesn't understand to a customer whose business he doesn't understand.

In addition to substantive knowledge, he must possess the traits that all good teachers have in abundance: enthusiasm, dedication, confidence. He must have the presence of an actor, the self-possession of a politician, and the conviction of a man of the cloth. As Tocqueville might have noted, those are attributes in generous supply in a democracy in which people are free and equal; and they become fully developed in organizations that prize them. It surprises people—but it shouldn't—that many of Xerox's best salespeople, both men and women, are former teachers.

Xerox and other marketing-oriented companies should be an unlikely future for young, bright teachers. Teaching should provide the same sense of adventure, entrepreneurship, and excitement that exists in our smartest companies. For the good of the country, let's hope that the schools of the future provide the kinds of challenges and opportunities that attract people to the private sector.

Money alone won't do it, and money alone shouldn't. Salary is important and teachers' salaries should climb, as long as they're subject to a market test. Equally important is the sense of satisfaction derived from the work itself. It's important to salesmen, and it's important to teachers. Good teachers love what they do and consider teaching a calling, a vocation. While that should never be used as an excuse to underpay teachers, we should never lose sight of the fact that teaching is a helping profession. A sense of efficacy and effectiveness is as important as income.

As the teaching profession matures, and the idea of board certification becomes a reality, teachers will need to learn to work in a wholly different environment, one in which master or mentor teachers oversee the work of apprentice or novice teachers, and one in which younger teachers continue to learn from more seasoned teachers. In the school of the future, the seasoned teacher will also discover that he has the same responsibilities the seasoned doctor has—he must take on the most difficult cases, and leave the easier, more routine work to junior colleagues. That means seniority will no longer provide an opportunity to get assigned to the easiest and most desirable schools.

Teachers will also have to learn that professionals live within a market and are subject to market discipline. That will be a demanding, but rewarding, experience, because schools of choice will mean that teachers are chosen, not assigned. The new profession of teaching will emerge from the world of a state monopoly characterized by compulsory attendance to a voluntary system with families choosing schools designed by the teachers and principals who work there.

Changes will occur, because today's schools provide a service called teaching. Tomorrow's schools will provide a capability called learning. The teacher of tomorrow will be dealing with a flexible-term, year-round magnet school in which students advance at their own pace. Teachers will be paid more and enjoy greater prestige. They will be experts in new learning technologies, and in the special relationships of machines and children in the classroom. In the classroom of the future, teachers will be coaches, and each child will have individualized computer instruction, offerred in part by "smart" computers, using artificial intelligence.

As the role of the teacher shifts and changes, so, too, will the role of the administrator. We have already advanced the radical idea that central administration should serve the schools, and not the reverse. To put some starch in that proposal, we argue that central administration should sell its services to the local school building. It's a serious recommendation, and it would have serious consequences. Administrators will have to pull their weight. They must begin to do so, because tomorrow's schools, like today's companies, must push decision making down the chain of command where it ought to be—with principals and teachers.

The most important administrator in the system, of course, is the building principal. The title used to be "principal teacher," and we think that it's now time to restore that role. In the school of the future, the principal will be the conductor of a medley of different instruments—orchestrating a blend of professionalism and technology as do today's most successful companies.

To date, teaching has been characterized by weak rewards and incentives, and equally weak disincentives and penalties. If you do little, no penalty is likely to attach to it, and if you do well, no reward is likely to attach to it, either. In the school of the future, market conditions will reward successful teaching and penalize unsuccessful teaching. And there can be only one measure of success: student performance.

5

Standards Are the Bottom Line

Only when student learning progress is comprehensively assessed, and matched against investments of money and time, can productivity be judged. Without such measurable productivity data, there is no rational way to modify the system to attain higher standards.
—Adam Urbanski,
President, Rochester Teachers Association and
Vice-President, American Federation of Teachers

AMERICA WILL FAIL to meet the competitive challenge if high standards are not set and met. It's that simple. The rest—all the hype and hoopla, all the talk about reform—will be for naught if standards are not raised. Use whatever metaphor you like. As we move into the twenty-first century, we need to break the education four-minute mile, hit sixty home runs in one season, rush a hundred yards a game.

The sad fact is that not enough is expected of American students. They have it too easy academically. Yet, we expect—and get—a good deal in athletics and other extracurricular pursuits. That's why we deliberately chose an athletic metaphor. In state after state, school district after school district, school after school, athletic performance is encouraged, rewarded, and honored. But academic performance is permitted to languish.

We cannot compete in a competitive world without the highest levels of academic success. If you doubt it, look at the competition. The Japanese, our most successful competitors, have the highest levels of educational achievement in the world. Japanese students have the highest test scores in the world. Indeed, Japanese students tend to cluster around the mean. In plain English, Japanese test scores are not the result of a large number of very high scores offsetting low scores, producing a high average. On the contrary, everyone scores relatively high.

Japanese students do so well on international comparisons because they go to school for a longer day than Americans and a longer year. They have—and do—more homework. They work harder. When a Japanese parent is asked why a student does well or poorly, the answer is invariably "effort." Ask an American parent the same question, and the answer is usually "ability." The Japanese parent thinks you work for success. The typical American parent thinks it's the luck of the draw.

As a consequence, a majority of American youngsters attend school 180 days a year while the Japanese student goes for 240. The typical American student has an hour or less of homework; the Japanese student two and one-half hours or more. The typical American suburban high school student works twenty hours a week in a fast food restaurant or similar place of employment. The typical Japanese high school student attends a *Juku*, an after school, private tutorial program designed to help the student get promoted.

What are the results of this remarkable system of education? On the plus side of the ledger, more than 95 percent of Japanese youngsters finish high school (even though attendance is compulsory only to age sixteen), and the student who completes Japanese high school has completed the equivalent of at least two years of a good American college. In addition to knowing how to read, write, and compute, the Japanese high school graduate understands complex instructions. He communicates easily with his colleagues on the shop floor, solves problems, and continues learning on the job. He is admirably prepared for world competition—he is part of the best prepared workforce in the world for mature production technologies, particularly export industries.

The Japanese workforce, at one level at least, is the envy of the world. There are negative sides, however. Japanese students are prepared for a life of intellectual discipline, but not for intellectual creativity. Japanese schools are extraordinarily rigid by American standards. School work is boring and monotonous, Rote memory, rather than inquiry, is the norm. Classes are large, and the Japanese teachers' union is dominated by communists. In short, it's not a system Americans would want to copy. But there is a lesson for us, and that is that the Japanese treat education as an instrument of national policy. They are convinced—as we should be—that without first-rate schools, they cannot have a first-rate economy. The Japanese secret was to design a school system consistent with their history, traditions, and culture. We can do the same.

Koichiro Ishii, the former CEO of Bridgestone Tires and a former student at Stanford University, was on Japan's National Council on Educational Reform. He greatly admires many aspects of American education. When asked what single reform he would implement if he could do only one, Mr. Ishii answered without hesitation, "I would introduce the Socratic method."

The answer speaks volumes, for it reveals both the sophistication and limitations of Japanese schools. Generally viewed as a relatively closed society, Japan is always ready to innovate and experiment, not to compromise Japanese culture and tradition, but to preserve them.

If the Japanese can do it, so can we. The price of high standards in America need not be conformity and sameness. To the contrary, we should keep what is best about our schools. The good ones are "loosely coupled organizations," to use the jargon of sociology. They are full of creative ferment. They encourage inquiry, exploration, innovation, entrepreneurship. That is the best of America, and we must preserve it.

To preserve it, however, we must raise standards, in precisely the way we have raised standards of athletic performance. The old records fall, because we have put our mind to improving performance. It's no accident that the four-minute mile barrier fell in 1954—Roger Bannister actually developed a plan to break it. What's true in track and field is true in every other sport. Records fall because people set out to break them, and as a consequence, performance across the board increases. Today, it's common for several runners in a mile event to finish well under four minutes, a feat that was thought to be impossible not long ago.

There's more at stake here than setting athletic records. Academic performance prepares people for full and rich lives as citizens, parents, friends, and workers. Academics set the stage for contemplation, introspection, artistic accomplishment. Mastery of academics should be a goal in and of itself, rewarding on its own terms. But it is instrumental, as well. It's through knowledge that we create wealth, cure disease, house the homeless, and feed the hungry. Education is the path out of subsistence and a life that is thoroughly "poor, nasty, brutish, and short," to quote the English philosopher Thomas Hobbes.

This sense of balance should pervade in the schools, and it should take one form in particular. We should not separate students into academic, general, and vocational tracks until the foundations of academic mastery have been laid. Schools should not prepare the academically talented—largely middle-class youngsters—for college and dump the working class and disadvantaged into vocational or general courses. It's a moral affront to consign our nation's children to two different futures, for that is exactly what dumping children into dead-end courses involves.

In fact, we are convinced that one of the reasons the dropout rate has stayed high for the past two decades is precisely because youngsters are smart—you can't pull the wool over their eyes. They know that the general and vocational curriculums are by and large a waste of time. They don't prepare students for meaningful work. Neither do they prepare them for postsecondary education. You can't fool students with a discounted and discredited diploma, which explains why nearly half of the 700,000 youngsters a year who don't complete high school on time eventually return to some institution to get a diploma or its equivalent. At some point, they begin to realize that a degree—any degree—is worth earning.

The logical policy consequence is to design a diploma, or set of diplomas, that mean something. If no one is fooled by the current diploma, design one that reflects real mastery, as is the case in French-speaking countries, for example. There, the diploma is so carefully calibrated that transcripts of record are not kept. Any education institution or employer knows precisely what a specific diploma attests to: a diploma *assez bien* (satisfactory) means one thing, a diploma *très bien* (very good) another, and so on. While precision of that kind may not be practical in the United States, it is possible to restore the meaning of diplomas.

First we have to set standards for a basic academic diploma to identify exactly what it is a student should know to earn one. It should be based on demonstrated mastery of a core body of knowledge, including the great documents of citizenship, history, literature, the principles of science and mathematics. Every child of normal intelligence, given enough time, hard work, and some degree of motivation should be able to earn such a diploma. There should also be an honors diploma for students of special accomplishment.

Either of those diplomas would require all students to master a course of study ordinarily thought of as college preparatory. Once it was thought that only the college bound could and should pursue such a course of study. In the days of the industrial economy, when tens of thousands of skilled and semi-skilled jobs existed all over the country, such an approach made sense. No longer. As we have repeatedly observed, the modern knowledge-based economy requires high levels of education for everyone.

As former labor secretary William E. Brock observed, not only are the jobs of the future more likely to require higher levels of education, the service jobs of the recent past and present require higher levels of education and sophistication. Brock emphatically stated that new employment in the service sector is not "McJobs."

Brock castigated the "prophets of pessimism, busily spreading a new myth about America's job situation." They concede that never has the rate of job creation been higher (13 million new jobs from 1982 to 1989), but they argue that they're not the right kind of jobs, meaning that they're service sector jobs, mostly part-time, dead-end, low-wage positions.

Brock pointed out that manufacturing and services need each other. They are not competing functions. "Remember," he urged, "the industrial sector isn't shrinking, except as a *percentage* of the work force, and that's not because it's getting smaller (it isn't), but because of the incredible boom in the service sector."

Most of the service-jobs-are-bad-jobs stories depend on which time period you examine. In the low-growth, high-inflation years, 1979 to 1981, the picture was not very bright. For the period from 1983 to 1986, the analysis changed rather dramatically. Inflation in the first four years was 10 percent, said Brock, and only 3.2 percent in the second. As a consequence, growth in employment in the second period was 3.4 percent, up from 0.1 percent, and real disposable income climbed from 0.7 percent to 3.7 percent. As Brock observed:

> We actually see a trend line rising rapidly toward opportunity, not sinking toward despair. . . . Much of the service sector consists of higher-paid work: transportation, public utilities, communications, finance, banking, insurance, and data processing. In the five years of recovery, only one major segment of the job market has declined: minimum-wage jobs have fallen 25 percent, while . . . jobs paying $10 an hour or more have increased by 50 percent.
>
> The fact is the number of jobs that require higher skills is growing much faster than those that require little education. The skills requisite to this new marketplace are cognitive reasoning, math, and communications.

In addition to fruitful employment, there are powerful political and social reasons to require a core curriculum for everyone. As E. D. Hirsch writes in his remarkable book, *Cultural Literacy*, the disadvantaged can't keep up, let alone compete, if we deny them access to content. The secrets of our culture are locked in the great works of the sciences and humanities. To imbue children with "process," to teach them "skills," rather than knowledge, leaves them intellectually impoverished.

A simple example makes the point. Professor David Berliner, former president of the American Education Research Association testified before the National Commission on Excellence in Education that in one state, Arizona, only 40 percent of the test items for the state-wide reading test actually were taught in the classroom. Is it any surprise that disadvantaged youngsters don't do well on such tests? Where are they going to learn the answers to test questions if they're not covered in school? Advantaged youngsters learn the answers at home, but does anyone believe that disadvantaged children can? That's precisely the nature of their disadvantage.

Everyone, then, should be expected to master a core curriculum, at least through age sixteen, preferably until age eighteen. And no one should be promoted without performance. That serves no one's purposes—not the class into which the student moves, not the student, not the school, not society at large. To fail to hold students to high standards is an act of cynicism that a democracy cannot afford. It works a cruel hoax on the student, and leaves everyone the poorer for it.

A core curriculum at first glance may appear to be inconsistent with what we have advocated in earlier chapters, namely choice and decentralization. We have also advocated letting teachers get more deeply involved in the choice of textbooks and tests. We realize that at a superficial level, that may sound contradictory, but it's not. It's a modern version of Nietzsche's notion that we must "reconcile freedom with necessity."

We believe that a core curriculum is necessary for a great continental democracy. We must speak a common language, we must be able to communicate with each other. And one of the most effective ways to assure that communication can take place is to have a common vocabulary of myth, anecdote, and fact. To know something about the great documents of citizenship is a prerequisite to assuming one's duties and enjoying the opportunities of citizenship. Every American should know and understand that the reciprocal of the right to a jury trial is the duty to serve on a jury if called. These are not simple ideas, yet they are within the grasp of every American—or should be. They are not ideas that should be limited to the academic track, restricted to the college bound. They are ideas that every American should be exposed to.

The core curriculum to which we refer is not intended to dominate every waking hour of students and teachers—to the contrary, we believe that it should be just that, a core, with room and time in the school day and year for other courses and activities. But the core curriculum must begin somewhere, and we think it should begin in elementary school. Elementary school should go beyond the three R's to include music, geography, history, and the beginnings of computer work—not computer literacy, but work with a computer. We also think that elementary school is the place to start mastering English and start learning a second language. In the global economy, language knowledge is essential.

Language mastery. What could be more important in the high-tech world of the postindustrial economy, the knowledge-based economy? Language mastery is the *sine qua non* of the modern democracy and the modern economy.

We can say without doubt and without fear of contradiction that fluency in English is essential for all Americans. It's essential for success not only in the United States, but also in almost every country in the world. Not since the Latin of the early church has there been a language so universal. Indeed, English, spoken by 500 million people, is the language of art, architecture, commerce, aviation, law, business, engineering, science, and medicine.

It's the first *or* second language of almost every educated person in the world. At this moment more Chinese are studying English than there are American citizens.

In the quantitative disciplines, for example, it's impossible to advance anyplace in the world without at least a reading knowledge of English.

What, in practical terms, does all this mean for our schools? Every graduate of every school in the nation must know how to read, write, speak, and understand *standard* English—anything less is to sentence the student to a life of hard labor. Black English, Creole, or other dialects will not do—they may be languages of artistic or cultural expression, and they are to be respected for that, but they are not the language of commerce or public discourse in a great continental democracy. To argue otherwise is a counsel of futility.

But what of the reality of Los Angeles, New York, and our other port of entry cities, where an absolute babel of foreign tongues fills the air? In Los Angeles alone, more than eighty languages are spoken in the schools. Tagalog, Cantonese, Thai, Farsi, Meo. Indeed, thirty years ago America's most common second language, Spanish, was only rarely heard outside the Southwest. Today, it's common in most of our great cities.

The issue of bilingualism—particularly Spanish-English bilingualism—is a heated political one, and we do not propose to reopen old wounds. But we do want to approach the issue from a business perspective.

Like free enterprise, language is a living thing, and it rises or falls according to its use, both as a medium of cultural expression and as a means of commerce. Knowledge of a foreign language can open many doors. Think, for example, of Marco Polo, the greatest trader of all time. He was a great trader because, among other things, he was a linguist. He resided at the court of the Great Khan because he literally spoke his language. Think of Cortez, whose conquest of Mexico was possible because of Malinche's role as translator of the Aztec. Without understanding his adversary, not even Cortez's considerable military skills would have sufficed.

Brad Butler, the former CEO of Procter & Gamble, one of the few American companies to do very well in Japan, speaks Japanese. And even he, despite his characteristic modesty, concedes the relationship between his knowledge of Japanese and P&G's success in that country. As Senator Paul Simon reminds us, you can buy in any language, but sell only in the customer's.

If the needs of commerce don't convince you, think of diplomacy and defense. When the Soviets overran Afghanistan, we had only one Farsi speaker in our Kabul embassy, and no Russian speakers.

Language can't be killed by statute, regulation, or constitutional amendment. Think of Franco's attempt in Spain to kill

Catalan, Basque, and Valenciano during his forty years of dicta-
torial rule. Those languages reappeared more vigorously after his
death. Closer to home, think of what Senator Simon calls "the
tongue-tied American" who must transact business throughout
the world. As he wryly notes, there are 10,000 Japanese businessmen who speak English, and fewer than 1,000 American
businessmen who speak Japanese. Is it any wonder the Japanese
do so well with their export industries?

Our point is a simple one—American ignorance of second
languages is woeful. It is a serious impediment to our continued
economic growth and an embarrassment internationally.

How does that fit with the question of bilingual education in
Los Angeles or any other place in the U.S.? As a people, we
should treat a second language as an opportunity, not a problem—a strength, not a threat. Treat the question of language
instruction as an academic and intellectual question, not an ideo-
logical one, and what was a liability becomes an asset.

Every youngster who comes to this country should master
English, but at the same time his or her knowledge of Farsi or
Spanish or Tamil or Cantonese should be considered an asset.
And every child who doesn't speak a second language should
have the opportunity to study one from first grade on. It's an
imperative in the modern world. Not only does it increase the
likelihood of our eventually developing cadres of Americans who
are bi- or even multilingual, but learning a second language has
sound pedagogical underpinnings, as well.

The study of a second language is one of the very best ways
we know to deepen the understanding of English. It's also a
window into another culture, something valuable in and of itself.
And it's a powerful means of increasing our appreciation and
understanding of our own culture.

At the high school level, the core curriculum should require
the *flexible term equivalent* of two years of the same foreign language and four years of English, three years of math and history,
two years of science, and one year of computer science. To some
readers, that will sound familiar and decidedly old-fashioned.
Indeed, to readers who attended academic high schools and
graduated before 1960, it will have a *déjà vu* feeling. For good

reason. It was the standard academic curriculum of the day, and we have brought it back with two notable exceptions: computer science and something we slipped in—*flexible term equivalent*.

The flexible term equivalent introduces a new concept of performance standards for students. We believe the traditional technique of organizing the curriculum around units of time, rather than units of accomplishment, must vanish. In college prep courses of the past, time—the class hour and the semester or quarter—was meant to be a proxy for content and mastery. Any student who had finished a three-unit course on a given subject was assumed to be as well prepared as any other student who had completed a similar course and earned the same grade. That has always been a polite fiction, and it has been abundantly clear for decades that there is little or no comparability among courses in similar schools, let alone among schools that are vastly different.

If advanced placement examinations can be used to award college credit—as they are—why can't high school students move through a specified curriculum at their own pace? The answer, of course, is that they can. There is no longer any reason to hold students—or teachers—hostage to the stopwatch and calendar. The modern curriculum can be designed for self-paced mastery.

The slow child can work slowly and deliberately. The quick child can move as rapidly as his talent and energy take him. Equally important, the quick or slow child on a particular day or with a particular problem can take his time, go back, circle the problem, surround it, finally master it. And it is likely that having done that, the slow child will find that he is not always slow, that he too has fast days or fast problem sets, just as the fast child knows he has slow days. Similarly, the newcomer, the immigrant, the child who has missed school because of illness—each will find flexible term equivalents a more rational and satisfactory way to move through school.

Skeptics should consider such straightforward courses as typing, the one vocational course every child should take. Historically, typing has been organized by the semester—a student takes so many hours of typing a day for so many weeks. Imagine teaching instrumental music the same way. The issue is not time, but mastery. Some students can learn to type in ten weeks, some will require fifteen, some twenty. It is really of no consequence how long it takes—what's important is speed and accuracy. Whether the student eventually gets a job in an office or becomes a newspaper reporter and uses a word processor all day long, it no longer makes a bit of difference if it took him six weeks or six months to learn to type sixty words a minute with 95 percent accuracy.

What's true of typing is true of every other course in the flexible term curriculum. Granted, it's harder to identify and measure performance in subjects like literature or science. It is clear that new tests and measurements will have to be developed to recognize achievement .

New flexible term criteria could free us from the tyranny of $20, machine scorable, true and false tests. They're a scandal, and they make us a laughingstock in the other developed nations that still rely almost exclusively on essay tests and oral examination. The American fascination with machine scorable tests such as the Scholastic Aptitude Test (SAT), and the American College Test (ACT) goes back to World War I and the need to induct large numbers of young men into the armed forces. We can also trace its roots to an obsession with the measurement of intelligence, an activity abused more than used in any helpful way.

The SAT and ACT were designed as aptitude tests to measure or identify youngsters with high ability. Their purpose was to overcome the bias of grades, old-boy networks, and the lack of comparability between schools, and to eliminate race, region, and social class as the determinants of college entry. (They are quite good at predicting college performance, but don't help much in overcoming background variables—middle-class children do best on the SAT and ACT.)

These tests have had a powerful influence on American schools. While they have rationalized college and university admissions, they have had a devastating effect on oral and written expression. They have replaced essay exams *and* oral exams. True and false tests don't measure command of written or spoken English, and as a consequence, writing and speaking ability has declined since the tests were introduced. That's an extraordinary irony, because never have speaking and writing ability been more important than in the postindustrial society.

The flexible term should render another education anachronism obsolete: the grading concept. The issue in typing, to return to our homespun example, is not whether you earn an A or a C, but how fast and accurate you are. Fifty words a minute with no mistakes? One hundred words a minute with a 30 percent error rate? Is that more or less useful than knowing that a student earned a B from a high school you never heard of?

The same is true of French, Russian, or Chinese. Would you rather know that a student earned A's and B's, or that he speaks, reads, and writes like a native? There's a second advantage, as well. Students who are measured by performance, rather than letter grades, accept the assessment more readily. They know it's more accurate and evenhanded, and they know that at some point they can improve their rating.

We are convinced that the only way the public school can survive in recognizable form is to adopt higher standards, performance ratings, and a core curriculum. The taxpaying public, the folks who pay the bills, will be willing to underwrite the costs of schools that work, schools they have confidence in. They will not underwrite schools that continue to fail.

Does the private sector have lessons about performance standards that are useful to the schools? The two most important lessons the corporate world can offer educators are accountability and measurement, both of which educators tend to view as millstones or worse. But accountability and measurement would define the terms of the student-teacher relationship and lay out expectations. No one prefers failure to success, and no one prefers to be a drone if he can be effective.

There must be clear objectives and hardheaded measurement of outcomes for an organization to succeed. One of the most important standards Xerox uses is one that any people-oriented organization can use effectively. Xerox has two customers, "external" and "internal." External customers need no explanation—they are the people and companies who buy or lease Xerox products. Internal customers are the people within the corporation who must pay their way as a part of serving external customers. Each division and department within Xerox must be able to identify its internal customers and provide them with the same kind of service external customers get. At Xerox, everyone has a customer for his work. No customer, no work.

What would that mean to the schools? The same thing, and it should be backed up with the accounting procedures necessary to give teeth to the idea. The central office's internal customers are teachers and building principals, and central administration—the most bloated part of the organization's budget—must respond to their needs.

In developing a new corporate culture, Xerox instituted a program called "Leadership through Quality." It has two dimensions: competitive benchmarking and employee involvement. Competitive benchmarking is a dynamic, continuous process to measure products, services, and practices against Xerox's toughest competitors *and* companies renowned for leadership.

It's a process at once very simple and very powerful. In every identifiable function, Xerox looks at the competition, to see both how well they are doing and what their rate of improvement is. It's not enough to know that they're doing well. Xerox must know precisely how well and how rapidly they are improving.

For example, as the Japanese successfully captured market share, Xerox's first analysis was that an annual productivity improvement of 8 percent in manufacturing would put Xerox back into a favorable competitive position. But that first analysis failed to take into account the rapidity of Japanese improvements. Upon re-analysis, it became clear that Xerox would have to increase its productivity performance by 18 percent per year to catch up and stay even.

But competitive benchmarking means more than looking at the competition in your own industry. It means looking at the best in *every* industry. Xerox has learned more about warehousing and distribution from L. L. Bean, the mail order retailer of outdoor clothing and gear, than it has from its own industry.

Competitive benchmarking may be the most important innovation in recent Xerox history, and we believe that it has major implications for America's public schools. Ideally, schools in an educational free market, competing for students and teachers, would be identifying the best competition they can find anywhere—across the street, across town, across the state, across the country.

For example, New York State and California, by virtue of population and scale, should regularly compare themselves with each other. And Los Angeles and New York City should compare themselves with their adjacent suburbs where the real competition exists for the more well-to-do parents. Both cities should compare themselves with other large urban districts with similar problems and opportunities, both to learn about programs that work and to remind themselves of their own successes.

Schools and school districts should also compare themselves with their toughest competition—private schools. And they should do so without complaining that private schools have all the breaks. Insofar as life may be easier for private schools, the public sector should identify in what ways and for what reasons their life is easier, and then seek remedies. Those remedies will involve making public schools behave more like private schools whenever possible (which is part of what choice is) and they will involve restructuring. But also needed are responses that are genuinely innovative from a public school perspective.

For example, public schools, at least until choice systems are fully implemented, should adopt academic bankruptcy procedures as a device to reorganize and reconfigure schools that are failing. A school that doesn't meet its minimum goals should be put on notice or fold.

And since sauce for the goose is sauce for the gander, public schools should also adopt management by exception as a prime tenet of school organization and performance measurement. All schools should be held to a minimum set of performance criteria, but these should be floors, not ceilings. Performance criteria should be an invitation to continue to raise standards, not to be satisfied once they are reached. Benchmarking with similar and better schools will help make that a reality. Management by exception should be used to deregulate public schools that regularly and significantly exceed minimum performance standards. Just as a bankrupt school should be put in receivership, an outstanding school should be permitted to escape the regulatory reach of the state.

For example, Palo Alto High in California, Boston Latin in Massachusetts, or Walt Whitman in Bethesda, Maryland, should be permitted to meet their goals without prescriptive state rules and regulations. They might be permitted to have waivers for teacher and administrator hiring practices, to use textbooks of their own choosing, or to adopt other practices that the school community thinks important and sensible. Doubters need look no further than the North Carolina School of Science and Mathematics. One of its strengths is its freedom from the regular provisions of North Carolina school law. The school uses textbooks of its own selection; hires teachers it thinks are good, without regard to state credentials; and generally operates as if it were a genuinely professional organization—which it is.

The truth is that prescriptive rules and regulations are necessary only in the absence of measurable performance objectives. Once there are performance standards, schools can be encouraged to do it their way in precisely the way corporations do. A corporate CEO expects his division chiefs and managers to innovate and improve on their own. Those that cannot are penalized, just the opposite of most schools today. At issue here are two points. Every school in the nation should set its sights higher but must also be realistic. A school in the inner city, with a long history of failure, should not be compared with a wealthy suburban school that sends most of its graduates to college—at least not in the beginning.

Similarly, a well-to-do suburban school should not be compared with a school in distress, for two reasons. If it does so it will be tempted to rest on its laurels, confident that it is doing well comparatively. But compared with what? A well-off school that compares itself with a poor school is living in a fool's paradise, because that is not the competition. The competition is another well-off school. Bronx Science should be compared with Stuyvesant in Manhattan, not a depressed school in the ghetto. Palo Alto High should be compared with Walt Whitman in Maryland.

The question of standards is ultimately a question of quality. Many observers have the mistaken notion that quality is more expensive than lack of quality. It's the "Rolls Royce" mentality. While it's true that Rolls Royces cost more, a poor-quality Rolls would cost even more. Xerox had to cross the bridge that the schools must now cross. Quality doesn't cost more—it costs less. When the Japanese were coming, Xerox and other corporations didn't understand that simple truth. It may cost more in the beginning to build quality in, but once it's built in it's virtually free. Quality spares the work of recall, which is always expensive. It increases customer satisfaction, which is a virtual guarantee of repeat business. It increases employee satisfaction. Quality is the original win-win formulation. But it's difficult for many managers to really act on that knowledge. Too often, they attempt shortcuts and improvisations that reduce quality and hurt long-term performance.

Xerox has made quality the cutting edge of its corporate strategy, but as good as it is, it's far from perfect. If Xerox did *everything* right the first time, it would save $2 billion a year— about 20 percent of revenues. The public schools' failure to teach children right in the first place costs society an enormous amount of money each year. The Committee for Economic Development estimates that each year's class of dropouts costs the nation more than $240 billion in lost earnings and forgone taxes over their lifetimes. Billions more will be spent on crime control, welfare, health care, and other social services.

It's essential to remember that quality control is a never ending process. In 1989 Xerox had reduced its component rejection rate to under 1,000 parts per million from as high as 8,000, but the Japanese rate was already consistently below 1,000. By 1991 the Xerox component rejection rate had fallen below 500 parts per million, but the Japanese had reduced their rejection rate to below 200. Knowledge of that kind is the spur to improving quality and output. It's a reminder that the job can always be done better and faster, at lower cost, and with higher quality.

The motto of a successful company or school must be: "We are no longer the organization we once were, but we are not yet the organization we want to be."

6

Values, Work, and Citizenship

Education does not mean teaching people what they do not know . . .
it is a painful, continual, and difficult work to be done by kindness, by
watching, by warning, by precept, and by praise, but above all—by
example.

—John Ruskin

OUR POLITICAL HERITAGE is a vision of liberty, justice, and equality. To perpetuate that vision, Thomas Jefferson proposed a general education not just for the privileged few, but for all "to enable every man to judge for himself what will secure or endanger his freedom." A generation later, Alexis de Tocqueville reminded us that our first duty was to "educate democracy." He believed in politics as the manifestations of the "notions and sentiments dominant in a people." Ideas, both good and bad, have their consequences in every area of a nation's life.

Today, the words of Jefferson and de Tocqueville take on a note of particular urgency. We are producing a generation of young Americans that neither understands nor appreciates our democratic society. They do not have the education to develop a solid commitment to those "notions and sentiments" essential to a democratic form of government.

Jack Beatty once wrote in the *New Republic* that "ours is a patriotism not of blood and soil, but of values, and those values are liberal and humane." Values are neither revealed truths nor natural habits. We are not born with them. Devotion to human dignity and freedom, equal rights for all, social and economic justice, the rule of law, civility and truth, tolerance of diversity, and self-respect must be taught, learned, and practiced. They cannot be taken for granted, or seen just as one set of options equal to any other.

Anyone who thinks it is possible to have a value-free education is dead wrong. Everything is not relative—there are constants in American life. Truth is still better than dishonesty, loyalty better than dishonor, fidelity better than infidelity, compassion better than lack of concern. Exclude values from schools and you teach children that values aren't important—they are. Historically, the schools, along with family and church, have been an important part of the transmission belt that carries values from one generation to the next.

Intellectually, values are the ordering principles by which we arrange and interpret the world around us. Values tell us what is important and unimportant, useful and useless. Students must know the difference between right and wrong, and those differences must be reflected in the life of the school. Academic standards and standards for behavior and demeanor are a part of education values. Students must recognize that there are penalties for improper behavior and rewards for proper behavior, just as there are rewards and punishments in the larger world.

Many will remember that those values were once present in public education. But somewhere along the line, values began to disappear from the curriculum of most schools. They disappeared first from the "visible" curriculum—textbooks and programs of study. Then they began to disappear from what we have described as the "invisible" curriculum, the messages teachers and administrators send to students about what is right and wrong, acceptable and unacceptable.

Imagine a school in which teachers and administrators let students earn course credit even though they are in class only three or four days a week. Imagine schools that issue diplomas for time served rather than real academic accomplishment. Practices of that kind send the wrong messages. They tell students that "anything goes," that standards of accomplishment and performance don't exist. American students may not be as well educated as they should be, but they're not dumb. They know when a school doesn't care about values and standards. It's the surest way to let students know you don't care about them. Schools that care hold students to high standards of behavior and performance.

That's especially true in the case of low-income and disadvantaged youngsters who are frequently dumped into the vocational or general track. The school is telling them they are not worth educating. Such practices are not only morally wrong, but over the long haul they represent a form of economic and social suicide. As we look to the next century, our workforce will be drawn increasingly from the poor and disadvantaged, many of whom are minorities and recent immigrants. They must be as well educated as their more fortunate brethren.

There is then both a moral and practical imperative for not consigning these youngsters to a dead-end education. The reality of the postindustrial economy is that dead-end schools produce dead-end lives. It's important for schools to teach values consciously, because the future of our nation depends on it. It's imperative that schools let all students know that they can learn and become productive members of society. And it's also important for schools to let youngsters know that values are important in and of themselves.

We are not alone in our concern. We both joined a distinguished group of Americans in 1987 as cosignators to *Education for Democracy: A Statement of Principles.* The report was issued by the American Federation of Teachers, the Educational Excellence Network, and Freedom House. Representing a growing consensus in this country that our schools should teach both moral and democratic values, the statement was signed by 150 educators, politicians, and business leaders, including William J. Bennett, then secretary of education; former president Jimmy Carter; Mayor Henry G. Cisneros of San Antonio; U.S. senator Bill Bradley of New Jersey; John J. Creedon, president and chief

executive officer of Metropolitan Life Insurance Company; Bill
Honig, California's superintendent of public instruction; and the
Rev. Theodore M. Hesburgh, president emeritus of the Univer-
sity of Notre Dame. The report says:

> We fear that many young Americans are growing up without
> the education needed to develop a solid commitment to those
> "notions and sentiments" essential to a democratic form of
> government. . . . Education for democracy must extend to
> moral issues. The basic ideas of liberty, equality, and justice,
> of civil, political, and economic rights are all assertions of
> right and wrong.

What values, then, should the school teach? We believe there
are three sets of values the schools must teach—democracy,
citizenship, and the workplace. If students don't have the opportunity to learn those principles in school, they won't have the
opportunity to learn them elsewhere.

Democratic values are the values of a free people who believe
in justice and equality. Toleration of differences, fairness, and
balance are all traits that should be part of the school, because
they are essential to life in a modern democracy. Students must
also understand that integrity, self-respect, and respect for others are essential in a democratic society.

The virtues of compassion, charity, equality, duty, and justice are integral to our concept of citizenship. Trial by jury is the
quintessential example. Citizens of a democracy must realize that
the reciprocal of the right to trial by jury is the obligation to serve
on a jury when called.

There is a more common, but no less important, set of values—
punctuality, neatness, and civility. They are the values of the
workplace, and they must be evident in the school. They demonstrate both respect for others and respect for one's self—two
qualities essential in the modern company, where human interaction and contact are the way of life.

From a business point of view, the values described above
are especially important, for the values of citizenship and a democratic society are also the values of a high-tech economy. Most
people don't think about values and business, except business

ethics. Are businesses honest and ethical? Those are important questions, and the Harvard Business School shouldn't be the first place to raise them. Values in school lay the foundation for values in the workplace. The nation has been shocked by revelations of criminal activity in the highest reaches of Wall Street. While Ivan Boesky's behavior can't be explained by school practices, business ethics should not be offered as an afterthought in an MBA program. Children should be expected to deal with ethical problems early in their lives.

If values and business cannot be separated, values and the schools cannot be separated either. Consider the study of history. There has been a sharp drop in the amount of time spent on history studies in American schools. Today, fewer than twenty states require students to take more than a year of history to graduate. Many students don't know about the prominent people and the central ideas and events that have shaped our past and created our present.

A recent study shows that a majority of high school seniors do not know what the 1954 *Brown* v. *Board of Education* decision was about. A majority couldn't identify Winston Churchill or Joseph Stalin. Without knowledge of our own struggle for freedom, how much can students understand about what it has taken and will still take to extend democracy at home? What can they know about democracy's capacity to respond to problems and to reform? Without knowing about World War II and its aftermath, how can they grasp the cost and necessity of defending democracy abroad? Without debating and discussing how the world came to be as it is, they won't know what's worth defending, what should be changed, and which political ideologies have to be resisted.

But the question remains—how should schools teach values? We believe that there are three tried and true methods that have withstood the test of time. They're used in the family, the workplace, private schools, and the nation's better public schools. They must be used in all our schools. They are study, example, and practice.

Study in school means a carefully selected curriculum, a systematic approach to subject matter. It involves the assignment of relevant textbooks, required reading, careful preparation, discussion, and debate. The values of citizenship emerge in our great works of literature. To impart such values, a modern core curriculum must include exposure to the historical documents of citizenship—*The Politics* and *Nichomacaen Ethics* of Aristotle, *The Republic* of Plato, *The Prince* by Machiavelli, *An Essay Concerning Human Understanding* by John Locke, *The Declaration of Independence*, the *Tenth Federalist Paper*, the *United States Constitution*, John Stuart Mill's *On Liberty*, the *Gettysburg Address*, and Martin Luther King's *Letter from Birmingham Jail*.

The key here is exposure. It would be too much to expect high school students to become experts in philosophy or political science, but they must be exposed to the documents of citizenship and expected to deal with their main concepts. Education requires dealing with a body of knowledge, facts, myth, history, anecdote, story. But education is not an exercise in memory alone—difficult material is to be mastered as an exercise in understanding, an exercise in critical thought. Through this process values emerge. Think of the centerpiece of the Fifth Amendment as simply a phrase to be memorized without understanding its underlying meaning:

> nor shall be compelled in any criminal
> case to be a witness against himself

Without understanding its purpose and historical context, it is empty. Why should a suspected criminal not have to testify against himself? Protecting all of us from testifying against ourselves emerged from a long and bitter history of the rack and thumbscrew—if a man may be compelled to testify against himself, who is to say no to the torturer? Certainly not the victim. Freedom from self-incrimination is no more and no less than freedom from the Inquisitor and the tools of his trade. It is a strange thing in a century so convulsed by violence of every kind that that simple truth is frequently overlooked when people "take the fifth." It is stranger still that schools don't teach such ideas.

History and context are important to education, because

they set the stage for the most important value school can impart: the value of clear thinking. People learn to think by thinking about demanding material. It is the essence of the Socratic dialogue, the most enduring and important teaching technique ever devised. The Socratic dialogue is mirrored in one other learning activity—when a student reads a demanding book, one that challenges and stretches the mind. That is why the choice of books in the curriculum is so important. Books embody the value systems that formal education must provide.

Mark Twain's *Huckleberry Finn* offers a particularly telling and appropriate example of values. It is so faithful to the American experience, it has become a part of it. It is a book for both the masses and the most discerning reader. Reading the book—and discussing it in class—requires sensitivity and discretion.

The book traces the human condition—the Mississippi is the River of Life, Huck the child of nature, Jim the victim of an oppressive and merciless society. The values it embodies are captured in Huck's monologue after he saves Jim from bounty hunters. As the bounty hunters are about to board the raft to look for the runaway slave, Huck tricks them into believing that the tent on his raft holds his sick father. Although he is successful, Huck is not elated:

> They got off and I got aboard the raft, feeling bad and low, because I knowed very well I done wrong, and I see it warn't no use for me to try to do right . . .

Huck continues in this vein, and then says,

> S'pose you'd 'a' done right and give Jim up, would you feel any better than you do now? No says I, I'd feel bad—I'd feel just the way I do now.

Huckleberry Finn glorifies the commission of a crime, because its purpose is moral: it is, among other things, an attack on slavery.

The power of the book is its values. To read *Huckleberry Finn* is to embark on an ethical and moral examination. It is hardly value free. It provides examples of courage, strength, and love. It shows the effects of hubris, greed, and the will to power. It reveals transcendent accomplishment and abject failure. Great books provoke the reader. They do so because they take ethical and moral positions. It is precisely those attributes that are the hallmark of great literature. Think of the *Iliad*, *Oedipus Rex*, *The Divine Comedy*, the tragedies of Shakespeare.

We expect there will be spirited and vigorous debate about which books should be included in the core curriculum. Such debate is healthy and welcome, but it should not obscure the fact that as a nation we need a common vocabulary to communicate effectively. E. D. Hirsch makes this point with power and elegance in his book *Cultural Literacy*. Recognizing that we risk criticism, we nevertheless propose to list ten books with which all Americans should be familiar. We begin with the Bible, not for theological but for cultural and literary reasons; we include, as well, *The Iliad*, *Hamlet*, *Gulliver's Travels*, *Moby Dick*, *The Education of Henry Adams*, *The Sun Also Rises*, *The Grapes of Wrath*, *Huckleberry Finn*, of course, and the collected poetry of Robert Frost. No great harm is done if a child reads a book that is not a classic. To deny children access to the classics, however, does do great harm.

Before the twentieth century, most Americans agreed that there was a common core of values that could and should be taught. It was embodied in the classical curriculum of the day. The disciplinary tradition of old still exists in the best public and private college preparatory schools. But for the most part, it has been virtually abandoned. Communications skills replace English, social studies replace history and geography. Is it any surprise that bachelor living and power volleyball have entered the curriculum?

Is it any wonder that there are periodic attempts to purge *Huckleberry Finn* from the classroom? With no intellectual and disciplinary anchor, the school is subject to the fads and vicissitudes of the moment. When the watchwords of the school become value neutral, everything is relative and anything goes. Nothing is imposed on anyone, except the notion that there are two sides to every question. The great revealed religions and the philosophy of the ancient Greeks, which believe in right and wrong and moral absolutes, no longer provide answers. Not even the existential answer that teachers know more than students can be offered with conviction.

There is one final concern with the idea of a core curriculum that must be addressed. Who will choose and what will the core consist of? It must be chosen by the wise and judicious, the penetrating and the discerning, the discriminating and the disciplined—in short, by you and me, not by rigid ideologues of the left or right.

The Committee for Economic Development's policy statement, *Investing in Our Children: Business and the Public Schools*, is the only education reform document we know of that deals with this issue explicitly. The trustees labored long and hard, first on the issue of a core curriculum, then on the issue of a national core curriculum. Their final report recommended that each state, not the federal government, identify and promulgate a core curriculum.

This provision would honor regional and local differences. The trustees were convinced—rightly, we think—that a national consensus exists that would spontaneously lead the boards of education in Florida and Maine, California and Minnesota, South Carolina and Oregon, to adopt a core curriculum that in all important respects would be identical.

Because of this reliance on the invisible hand of a shared culture, no bitter political battle would be fought at the national level over the issue of a national curriculum. Indeed, we already have a *de facto* national curriculum. The Educational Testing Service, through its achievement and advanced placement examinations, is easing us slowly and painlessly into one.

We have discussed at length *study* as the first way of learning and teaching values, because we believe that the core curriculum introduces and embodies values. But equally important is *example*, particularly the teachers' own behavior and attitudes. If teachers believe and behave as if the values contained in the books they assign are important, students will take the message to heart. Indeed, that is one of the most important reasons for increased professionalism for teachers.

The most famous case of teacher-as-example is Socrates. He drank the hemlock cup, not because he was guilty of corrupting the youth of Athens, as he had been charged, but to demonstrate the supremacy of the law.

There are less dramatic examples than Socrates'. The good teacher is not just didactic. The good teacher is a living lesson. The good teacher embodies the pleasures and satisfactions found in disciplined inquiry and mastery. Students lucky enough to have teachers who really care about the life of the mind will have that sense of excitement indelibly imprinted on them.

But there are also the day-to-day examples of life in the school. Schools where teachers and administrators respect learning set a lasting example for students. And schools that effectively communicate the importance of self-respect and self-discipline in student leaders help communicate that to other students, particularly newcomers, younger students, and transfers. They are important examples for life after school. They remind students that there isn't something called school and something else called the real world. It's all real, and school should not be exempt from the kinds of demands that the workplace and the larger society impose.

Finally, there is the question of *practice*. "Happiness," Aristotle tells us, "is activity of the soul in accord with perfect virtue." And we achieve that state by practice. It's not so much in the exercise of our rights that we learn that, but in meeting our obligations.

At the level of friend and family, it means satisfying the reciprocal demands that loyalty and filial responsibility place upon us. At the level of the community, it means meeting minimal standards of civility and good conduct, not just obeying the law, though that is important, but also accommodation to unspoken standards of behavior. At the level of the state, it means honoring the demands of citizenship—honesty in paying taxes, voting and citizen participation, and in time of mortal danger, it may mean the ultimate sacrifice for a higher good.

At the level of the school, practice means just what it suggests—doing what is expected of you and doing it well. But it should mean much more. It should mean service, both to the school and to the community. We have already mentioned one of the most important education reforms of the past decade, the

North Carolina School of Science and Mathematics created by Governor Hunt in the late 1970s. It is known across the country as one of only a handful of public boarding schools. It is devoted to demanding study and enrolls some of the best and brightest youngsters in North Carolina.

It is distinguished academically and socially, and its eight admission criteria produce a student body that is representative geographically, ethnically, and racially. It is among the nation's leading producers of National Merit Scholars. But what is special about this school is a unique graduation requirement: no student may graduate without performing three hours a week of school service and four hours a week of community service. Students from NCSSM spend time in nursing homes, orphanages, day care centers, and hospitals. They work with the elderly, the infirm, the disabled, and the dispossessed.

Every high school student in America could also be expected to perform community service as a condition of graduation. No one is so poor or elevated as not to profit from it. They would be learning—through practice—habits of service, the very foundation of civic virtue.

Other examples of practice are so numerous and obvious that they need not be belabored. Suffice it to say that anything worth doing requires practice, whether it's playing a musical instrument, speaking a second language (speaking one's first language for that matter), driving a car, or playing golf. Each of those activities is imbued with value—the value of hard work, self-discipline, constancy, and finally, mastery. There are no shortcuts to mastery, no tricks.

There are also important examples of practice that we take for granted. In most American schools, democracy is practiced from the earliest grade. Class officers are elected, committees are formed, deliberation and debate go forward. To use a phrase from political science, not partisan politics, those are "republican virtues." Men and women who are free and equal discuss, debate, and vote. If that process begins as early as grade school, it is deeply ingrained by adulthood.

We recognize that there is tension in our proposals. On the one hand we suggest that we adopt a core curriculum—what we need to know as Americans, to have both a shared sense of community and a shared destiny. At the same time we advocate market differentiation—choice among different schools. But we believe choice and core curriculum can be reconciled. Magnet schools and private schools are already doing it. Why can't all our public schools have the benefit of both?

We close this chapter with a brief discussion of religion and the public schools. We believe that in a pluralistic democracy, which prizes religious freedom and toleration, and which believes in the separation of church and state, public schools cannot be the salesmen for any particular religion. Does that mean, however, that they must be silent on the issue of religion?

One aspect of religion and values that deserves special attention in our schools is their intellectual history. We mean to distinguish between religion as state-sponsored or state-condoned worship, and religion as a form of human experience, insight, and understanding. A curriculum that is silent on religion is both dishonest and anti-intellectual.

Unhappily, many American schools and textbooks *are* silent about religion, as though by ignoring it, religious freedom might somehow be protected. That's a false notion altogether. History cannot be understood if religion is ignored. Most American textbooks, for example, don't even mention that Martin Luther King was a Baptist minister. That's not a way to keep religion out of the classroom. It's simply dead wrong. Even worse, it sends the wrong message to young people. It suggests that an incomplete and incorrect story is acceptable and sufficient. It's not. The greatest domestic event of this century is the civil rights movement, and it can't be fully understood without teaching and appreciating its religious foundations.

Government did not spearhead the civil rights movement. Government was the object of the civil rights movement. In the beginning, at least, government was the villain. The black churches of America led the civil rights movement, with the passionate conviction that it was a moral crusade. So strongly did King and his followers feel, they were prepared to challenge the established legal order. They were willing to go to jail to demonstrate the strength of their beliefs. They bore religious witness to the justice of their cause, and in so doing, exposed the law as invalid.

That, in abbreviated form, is the moral history of the civil rights movement, and for a book or teacher to fail to include a discussion of its religious component is simply wrong.

Schools should not proselytize on religion and morality, but neither should they ignore religion and its important role in history. The religious experience is provided by the family and church. At least some knowledge of religion should be imparted by school. Just as a diverse, pluralistic people needs a solid core of knowledge and skills, we need a people grounded in a solid core of ethical values.

7

The Federal Role:
Uncle Sam
Goes to School

The worth of the state, in the long run, is the worth of the individuals composing it.

—John Stuart Mill

THROUGHOUT OUR HISTORY, education has been a local and state responsibility—but it has always been a national concern. From the time of the Founding Fathers, thoughtful Americans have been interested in education from a national perspective. They have questioned what the federal role in education should be, and how much money the federal government should spend on it.

That pair of questions is especially important in light of the United States Constitution. Because the Constitution is silent on the education, the Tenth Amendment, the Reserve Powers clause, takes precedence: Any power not specifically mentioned as belonging to the federal government is reserved for the states. Education is thus a state responsibility, and the fifty state constitutions deal with it explicitly and often at length.

As a result of the Tenth Amendment, the federal government cannot *compel* states to participate in education programs. It can entice them, it can cajole them, it can encourage them, but it cannot compel them. Federal education programs cannot be mandated. They can be funded, and the funding may be attractive enough to attract state participation, but the state cannot be forced to participate.

That general observation, it must be clear, is about education programs, not civil or consititutional rights. The federal government enforces the constitutional guarantees we all enjoy. But Washington has no control—indeed, can have none—over other aspects of education. The federal government requires states and localities to treat all citizens equally—black and white, Anglo and Hispanic, able-bodied and handicapped—but it cannot dictate curriculum content, teacher licensing standards, or rules for homework or grades.

States and localities make the important decisions about who teaches, what they teach, in what circumstances schools will be operated, and what the conditions of advancement and matriculation will be. As long as the civil rights of students are observed, Washington is satisfied.

Local school districts are agents of the state, creatures of state government and state policy. The state may delegate substantial authority to local districts, including taxing authority, but in the final analysis, the state calls the shots. While there is substantial variety from state to state (Hawaii has a single statewide school district, and New Hampshire is highly decentralized), the state-local relationship is very different from the federal-state relationship.

The relationship between Washington and a state capital depends—in most cases—on money. How much money, in what program configuration, determines whether the states will accept federal funds—which is to say, whether they will participate in federal programs. Generally, states participate and do so willingly. The Congress is elected from the states, and few representatives are prepared to vote for legislation that might hurt their home district. It is, by and large, a sensible system.

Local control makes pedagogical, as well as political, sense.

It's clear, in education as in many other things, that small is better than big. The sense of intimacy, of belonging, of participation that goes with small schools and small school districts, is an invaluable educational asset. The one thing small units don't produce, however, is economies of scale. What can Washington do that the states and localities cannot do at all, or cannot do as well?

To answer that question, it is necessary to look briefly at what Washington has done to date. Most Americans agree that there should be a federal role. Indeed, most Americans are used to it. In the mid-nineteenth century, federal land was made available to the states if they were prepared to build and create institutions of higher learning. Land grant colleges are an enduring monument to this day, numbering among their ranks some of the nation's great state universities—those in Wisconsin, Michigan, Indiana, and Ohio, to name only a few. Originally founded to advance the art and science of agriculture and animal husbandry, as well as the practical arts and sciences of engineering and home economics, the mission of the original land grant institutions has been enlarged to include the whole sweep of human knowledge.

The only other federal program to equal the land grant college program in size or impact was the Serviceman's Readjustment Act, or GI Bill. Enacted as World War II drew to a close, it elicited furious opposition, as well as enthusiastic support. Robert Maynard Hutchins, then president of the University of Chicago, said it would turn institutions of higher learning into "intellectual hobo jungles."

How wrong he was. Never in history has a single education program meant so much to so many. Never has it meant so much to a nation's well-being, either. The truth is that the GI Bill was a massive investment in human capital, an investment of a size and scope never before contemplated. It was the single most important element of the stunning post-war recovery, because it introduced scores of thousands of former GIs, first to learning, then to work. It was the domestic counterpart of the Marshall Plan. Former GIs were students without peer—seasoned and wiser. They were eager to make their mark in the new world that awaited them after the allied victory.

It's important to remember, as we think about the future, that there was a strong element of fortuity about the impact of the GI Bill. The president and the Congress knew that as victory drew near, demobilization would eventually become a reality. Yet, everyone feared a return of the Great Depression. In structural terms, the GI Bill looked as much like a welfare program as an education program. To be eligible, you had to be a veteran. To draw benefits, you had to be a student. Where you studied and what you studied were up to you. Because of the sheer size of the program, individual benefits were paltry, even though aggregate expenditures were enormous. As far as the individual student was concerned, the GI Bill was mere subsistence. GIs, their spouses, and children lived with very limited financial resources, confident only that their education would pay off in the end. It did, and handsomely, for them and for American society as a whole.

The next important federal education program was the War on Poverty, part of Lyndon Johnson's "Great Society." Johnson's promise was as old as America. Education would be the way out of poverty. The poor and dispossessed would use education as the avenue to a better life for themselves and their children. And while the results of the War on Poverty were mixed, it spelled the difference between education and no education for some people. In particular, Pell Grants (for needy college students) and guaranteed student loans (for the less well off) meant that higher education was possible. Title 1 (now Chapter 1) aid to the disadvantaged has had a less dramatic success story to tell, but its purposes were the same—to empower the dispossessed. PL 94-142, which provided aid to the handicapped, was a signal from the Ford administration that the reach of federal civil rights protections would be expanded.

The federal role, then, is both old and new, dating back to the Founding Fathers, and ebbing and flowing to the present.

Today, with massive budget deficits, and fierce competition for federal dollars, there is little likelihood of increased federal spending for education. It is not our intention here to argue for a greatly expanded federal role. But we are convinced that existing federal expenditures can be targeted more effectively, and that

small, carefully orchestrated increases can be designed and justified without busting the budget. There is, in fact, widespread
agreement on both sides of the aisle that the federal role should
remain, but it must be sharpened and improved.

Education, however, will have to prove itself anew and demonstrate to the public that there is a payoff, an education bottom
line. That's a challenge American educators should meet with
anticipation and excitement, because evidence demonstrates that
education pays, and it pays handsomely. We know that educated
people and societies with high levels of educational attainment
do well. As we have seen with the Japanese, education can be an
instrument of national economic policy.

The issue for us should not be more dollars for old programs,
it should be more education for the same dollar—with new standards of performance and accountability. It is by now an old saw,
but true nonetheless: There will be more dollars for education
when there is more education for the dollar. The American public
has been generous. Not only do we spend more on education
than any nation in the world, our rate of increase has been
unparalleled. It will continue, but only if the public is convinced
that it is getting value for its tax dollar.

The 19th Annual Gallup Poll of the Public's Attitudes toward
the Public Schools, commissioned by the *Phi Delta Kappan* magazine in 1987, made that point powerfully. Eighty-four percent of
the American public thought the federal government should require states and localities to meet minimum federal standards. At
the same time, the American public thought the role of the federal government should be limited, and that education is funda-
mentally a state and local responsibility.

To many, that sounds inconsistent—should the federal government enlarge its role or not? We think those positions are not
inconsistent. They correspond with American history and tradition. They are only inconsistent if you are wedded to an outmoded model of top-down command and control and hierarchical management of a vast bureaucracy.

That model of bureaucracy worked for American industry in
the heyday of manufacturing and extraction, but no longer.
Doubters should look at the serious problems American industry

encountered in the sixties and seventies as more flexible, leaner, and responsive competitors entered the fray. Successful firms downsized, cut middle management, listened to the customer, and delegated responsibility to the lowest possible level in the organization.

In that scenario, the worker becomes a willing and productive participant. The analogy with the schools is nearly perfect. The same Gallup poll showed that schools that are most liked are those in small cities and towns. They are schools on a human scale, institutions we can all relate to. Schools that get lowest marks are those in large cities of the Northeast, and the citizens who give them the lowest marks are inner-city minorities. Why? Because those minorities have the most riding on school quality—the most to lose if schools are bad, the most to gain if they are good. Inner-city blacks, Hispanics, and poor whites have no coupons to clip, few networks to tie into. Education for them is serious business. Yet they are the most educationally disenfranchised of all our citizens.

As we suggested in the chapter on choice, one of the most important aspects of a choice system will be to re-enfranchise the dispossessed, give them power over their own lives, and invigorate community groups with a sense of real purpose. But what, one may ask, do those issues have to do with the federal government? Washington doesn't run schools. Indeed, the federal share of financing averages less than 8 percent.

One of the most important things that Uncle Sam can do is provide a "bully pulpit." You may have disagreed with the Reagan administration's positions on education issues, but no one can ignore the fact that it changed the agenda and raised the public's consciousness about education.

Each level of government should do what it does best. Washington doesn't run schools, because it can't. Running schools, to use the jargon of both business and public administration, exceeds Washington's span of control. Local districts run schools, because they are better at it than higher levels of government. And some local districts are very good, indeed. It's clear that the very best—districts like Montgomery County, Maryland; Palo Alto, California; and Wellesley, Massachusetts—know more about education, and how to address educational issues, than any other level of government.

The school districts that are not good at education are typically very poor or very big. Poor districts, by definition, have a difficult time, because they don't have the resources to serve their student populations adequately. No less a problem, however, are the giant school districts, the dinosaurs of the modern era. The nation's largest district, New York, with nearly one million students, is larger than the total enrollments of thirty-seven states. Los Angeles City Unified, with well over a half-million children, is larger than twenty-six states.

The nation's largest 600 districts enroll 40 percent of the nation's children. We are convinced that those districts present many of the same problems the federal government does—size and scale are barriers to excellence when they become dominant and infiltrate day-to-day operations. Size and scale are assets only when they serve the small units that make up the larger entity.

Size and scale work to Washington's advantage in one very important area. Only the federal government has the financial resources and the overarching national interest to support a sustained research effort. This is particularly true with basic research, where costs are high and the payoff unsure. But even applied research is most efficiently supported at the national level. Lessons learned about computers, reading instruction, testing and measurement, and organizational theory would pay off in all schools.

One important barrier to R & D at the state and local level is the free rider—the school district waiting in the wings for someone else to pay for education research, because once the results enter the public domain, they are free for the taking. We're not suggesting that school boards and superintendents conspire to avoid paying for research. We are simply pointing out that there are few incentives to support research, and there are many free riders.

In the business world, companies that have very large financial bases and enjoy very strong market positions have to underwrite significant research if they are to survive, let alone prosper. The issue in the modern economy is the generation of knowledge, because today, as never before, knowledge is power. Knowledge is what high-tech companies sell. It may look like they're selling hardware—copiers, or PCs, or printers, or mainframes—but they're selling solutions to problems. They're selling ideas.

Xerox regularly spends 5 to 7 percent of revenues a year on research and development. In 1990, it was $848 million. The federal government's education research budget is under $100 million, less than 15 percent of Xerox's research budget. In the high-tech world, low levels of R & D investment are an invitation to disaster. The important word here is investment. R & D is not an operating cost, though it may come out of an annual operating budget. R & D is the future.

No single feature of the education system is more shocking to business leaders than low levels of education research spending. The CED report, *Investing in Our Children: Business and the Public Schools*, states:

> Private industry could not succeed with a data collection system and research base as weak as this nation has in the field of education. Yet, it is only through education research and data collection that we can expect to identify ways and means to increase the output of the education system. The original purpose of a federal role in education was as a national repository of information, and the first federal Department of Education, launched in the 1860s, was designed to accomplish that objective.

Put slightly differently, the nation's education research expenditures are less than one-tenth of 1 percent of the national expenditure for education operations and capital outlay, which in 1987 was approximately $150 billion. Can you imagine where American companies would be in the competitive scheme of things if they behaved in the same way? Education research is so inconsequential that it doesn't warrant a line item in the federal budget summaries. The U.S. government spends more on agricultural research than it does on education research. We know more about pork bellies and soybean futures in this country than we do about our schools.

Only one federal program measures educational achievement on a regular basis, the National Assessment of Educational Progress, or NAEP, the "nation's report card." As important as NAEP is, it's a slender reed to lean on. The government gives NAEP $4 million a year—about ten cents for every child in public school, a sum so paltry as to be an embarrassment. It's no wonder we know so little about academic performance across the nation, and that we have very little confidence in the information we do have.

Unfortunately, educators have to take much of the blame for this perilous state of affairs. Many, if not most, of the education interest groups resisted efforts like NAEP's to collect the kind of data that would make meaningful comparisons possible. Shocking as it may seem, the attitude of the education interest groups was "ignorance is bliss." To their credit, most of them have finally changed their public positions on the matter and now support more data collection. The most important breakthrough is the willingness of the Council of Chief State School Officers to finally accept state-by-state comparisons, which they once adamantly opposed.

NAEP's 1992 budget request is $28.1 million, more than a threefold increase over its 1989 budget of $9.4 million. NAEP's new budget should be only the first step in a new federal R & D role. It should be possible in the nineties for educators, informed laymen, legislators, governors, and policy analysts to make straightforward and meaningful comparisons about their schools. We look forward to the day when governors will boast about the academic accomplishments of their students as much as they do now about prowess on the football field.

Interest in education research is not restricted to the public sector. Xerox, for example, believes it has a natural and legitimate stake in knowing what makes education productive, how people learn, and how technology can be applied to education. In the fall of 1986, Xerox established a nonprofit learning institute that is using artificial intelligence to study how people think and learn.

It's called the Institute for Research on Learning. It's associated with the Xerox Palo Alto Research Center—PARC, for short—and the University of California's Graduate School of Education at Berkeley. Xerox invested $5 million to get the program off the ground.

The institute is trying to merge new theories of learning with new breakthroughs in microprocessor technology and artificial intelligence, the programming technology that gives computers knowledge and reasoning power to reach conclusions the way humans do. One of the institute's first priorities is to study the concept of apprenticeship and collaborative learning, and to create learning environments to support it. Down the line, Xerox hopes that the institute will be able to develop personalized learning systems that build on a student's own thought processes and experience.

For all the examples of R & D that the private sector will undertake on its own, there remains much to be done by the public sector. Public elementary and secondary schools enroll more than 85 percent of the nation's youngsters, and their education requires a sustained commitment to publicly funded education R & D. We know a good deal about how to improve the education of children. What remains to be done is disseminate those findings to those who would profit from them and provide the resources to put them into practice. Research already demonstrates our conviction that genuine reform must begin in the local school building. That's where education takes place, where the talent is, and where good practices must be adopted and strengthened.

What can the federal government do about this? We believe a venture capital fund should be established to encourage and permit locally initiated experimentation and innovation—by teachers, principals, and their school communities. Both the states and school districts should be bypassed in favor of the school building. That idea, of course, is consistent with our earlier exposition about magnet schools and schools of choice, as well as school site budgeting and deregulation. But even if those ideas are not adopted immediately, the federal government should create a venture capital fund for schools.

How should the fund be financed, and how should it be run? For starters, we propose that $1 a student be the target—$40 million in the first year. That amount should be increased if the program is a demonstrated success. How would it be run? The secretary of education would create an advisory panel of teachers and principals to give advice on the procedures and policies, as well as the amount and duration of individual grants.

Teachers and principals from local schools would submit proposals to the secretary, and awards would be made to schools only—not school districts. They need not be large awards, and the paperwork to win one shouldn't be burdensome. Educators should take a page from the experimental scientist's book: In real science, most experiments fail. Only the exceptional experiment succeeds, but with careful research protocols, the scientist learns from both successes and failures.

Albert Shanker told us that the biggest problem with research in education is that all experiments are "doomed to succeed." He was half joking—but only half—and we think he hit on a sensitive point. No one wants to fail where a student's future is at stake. Equally important, in the world of education grants, a failed project means no more funds. If that were true in the hard sciences, research would grind to a halt. What is clearly needed with any venture capital fund is a corresponding set of program reports and evaluations that would not eliminate weak projects, but would inform the process of education research and analysis.

Woody Allen, probably the greatest American humorist of our day, says only two out of ten of his jokes work. Xerox defines its success rates in these terms: Only 10 to 20 percent of research time and dollars ultimately lead to a product or a product improvement that's brought to market. But Xerox is very pleased with that ratio. Good R & D is one of the few areas—if not the only one—where failure breeds success. That's why good corporate R & D is willing to take risks and go down roads that often look like dead ends.

Sometimes, you need a long series of research dead ends to get solid results that can make a real difference. Chester Carlson struggled for more than ten years to develop the xerographic process. It took Xerox twelve more years to produce the first plain-paper copier, the Xerox 914. What business expects from education research is more of that kind of curiosity, more of that kind of risk taking, and more money to do it with.

In addition to the venture capital fund of $40 million, the federal government should put funds behind the idea of magnet schools of choice. In the first instance, magnet schools were largely a federal creation, driven by necessity and inventiveness. As involuntary busing became more and more unpopular with both minority and majority parents, and as housing patterns shifted in our central cities, it became apparent to many that the ideal of racial integration was receding ever further. Magnet schools were a device to increase voluntary racial integration by creating schools that would be so appealing that youngsters of all races and socioeconomic backgrounds would willingly attend them. By and large, they've worked. Racially integrated magnet schools are able to turn their energies and attention to curricular and other issues.

Federally funded magnet schools are the great unsung success story of federal aid to education. There is no reason to think that more cannot be done with the same approach. We believe the federal government should establish a program of matching funds to local schools and school districts to establish more magnet schools. Grants averaging $50,000 per district, matched locally, would provide the resources to begin the process of moving into magnet schools on a large scale.

Critics will argue that $50,000 is not enough. They may be right, but the realities of the present budget crunch are such that it would be difficult to find more. Moreover, there is a point at which a granter can be too generous; $50,000 may not be that point, but it's clear that for a reform to work, it must be the product of local initiative and enterprise—$50,000 is small enough for local initiatives to match. Washington can't buy reform. All it can do is set the stage for reform to occur.

We believe, as well, that there is a role for Washington in the preparation of teachers, one that we think dovetails with an old, as yet untried, idea in this country—national service. Washington could forgive all or part of the college loans of young people who become teachers in hardship areas or who teach specialties in short supply. For each year of service, they would get one year of loan forgiveness. Conventional economists will protest that the cost of preparing teachers should not be hidden in an obscure subsidy program, that other more explicit inducements should be used to get young people into teaching. We disagree.

Teaching is in part a calling, a vocation. It never has been, and never will be, a "get rich" profession. This is not an excuse to pay teachers too little. It's a reminder of what teaching and other helping professions really are. Inducing young men and women to teach who might otherwise not consider it, particularly in hardship areas, is a social policy worth pursuing for its own sake. Subsidizing the loans of those teachers is a small price to pay.

Finally, there is a strong national consensus that it is the federal government's responsibility to take the lead in combating poverty and to provide educational assistance to disadvantaged children. The federal government for the past two decades has had two special programs for the poor and the disadvantaged—Head Start and Chapter 1.

While considerable evidence demonstrates that both programs have been effective, funding levels have been inadequate. The biggest problem with Head Start and Chapter 1 is that they reach far too few eligible children. Head Start, for example, enrolls only about 440,000 children—fewer than one out of every five eligible youngsters. And Chapter 1 services reach only about half of all eligible children.

Washington has to fully fund Head Start and Chapter 1 programs so they reach every single eligible youngster. The Congressional Budget Office estimates that to fully fund these programs would cost $10 billion to $12 billion per year, a significant but not impossibly large number. It's within reach, particularly if program effectiveness can be documented.

We believe that there are both moral and pragmatic reasons for such an increase. Morally, the richest society on earth cannot ignore the least among us. We cannot let children fail, for that is surely their fate without such programs.

If the moral grounds are not compelling enough, the pragmatic grounds are. Changing demographic trends and social realities indicate that educating those youngsters to take their place in the American mainstream is absolutely critical to our ability to compete in the future.

As Harold L. Hodgkinson points out in his study, "All One System," published by the Institute for Educational Leadership, "In 1955, 60 percent of the households in the U.S. consisted of a working father, a housewife mother, and two or more school-age children. In 1980, that family unit was only 11 percent of our homes, and in 1985 it was 7 percent, an astonishing change."

The demographics are frighteningly clear. Sixty percent of the children born in 1983 will live with only one parent before reaching age eighteen—that now becomes the normal childhood experience. Of every 100 children born today:

- Twelve will be born out of wedlock.
- Forty will be born to parents who divorce before the child is eighteen.
- Five will be born to parents who separate.
- Two will be born to parents, one of whom will die before the child is eighteen.

In addition to the distractions and psychological traumas likely to result from such family disruptions, single-parent homes are statistically more prone to occur in lower-income families. Among black children today, almost half grow up in single-parent homes headed by females, and half grow up in families whose incomes are below the poverty line.

Growing up in poverty is statistically correlated to higher levels of dropping out of school, poverty in later life, less likelihood of a stable work life and sufficient income level, and more likelihood of involvement in criminal or other antisocial activities.

We think the evidence of ruined lives is compelling, and that intervention strategies that seek to solve a problem before it gets acute are preferable to intervening after the problem appears full blown. That kind of intervention can have a profound and positive effect on our economy and our ability to compete.

Our favorite example to bolster that argument is a study of 100 children in Ypsilanti, Michigan, between 1962 and 1967. All 100 children were from poor minority families, and all were considered to have low IQs. Half of the children were randomly assigned to a preschool program. The other half were not. Both groups were carefully monitored for fifteen years.

The results clearly demonstrate the importance of preschool activities for disadvantaged children. The group that took part in the preschool program was twice as likely to hold a job or be in college or in a vocational training program as those who did not. They graduated from high school at rates a third higher than the other group. Their arrest rates were 40 percent lower, and teen-age pregnancy rates were almost half. More importantly, they were 50 percent more likely to score at or above the national average on tests designed to measure functional competence.

While Chapter 1 compensatory programs may not show such dramatic results, there have been enough indications to suggest that they, too, can be a crucial factor in helping many youngsters stay in school and make their way into the mainstream. Some experts suggest that the recent rise in measured black achievement on national standardized tests can be traced to the effects of Chapter 1 programs. Such programs represent an investment in our future. They show how a federal education program can work well, without imposing federal bureaucracies or control on local schools.

Washington should fully fund Head Start and Chapter 1 programs so they reach every single eligible youngster. The need is so crucial, we think the money must be found. It is hard to imagine that it cannot be squeezed out of a trillion-dollar federal budget. In the long run we will save tax dollars. Every dollar invested in quality preschool programs can return almost $5 in lower future costs of special education, public assistance, and crime prevention. An annual $500 investment in compensatory education can save the cost of a student repeating a grade— estimated at about $3,000. Any business would be pleased with a return on investment of 400 percent to 600 percent, and when such yields are available through federal investments in the human resources our young people represent, they should be made without hesitation. And if the likelihood of higher lifetime incomes and payment of taxes on those incomes is factored into the equation, it becomes absolutely irresponsible not to invest in fully funded preschool and compensatory education.

Put bluntly, the well-off and well educated are not replacing themselves. The only way our economy can grow and expand—something that benefits us all—is to develop those youngsters into tomorrow's workers. Indeed, for that very reason the American business community is critically interested in public education. Although not in the position to mandate education solutions, Washington can target funds and establish partnerships. More important, it can provide leadership as a powerful, honest, and concerned broker.

As things now stand, the business community is being asked to do the school's product recall work for them. Students who leave school unable to read and write, unable to communicate, unable to meet the social obligations of the modern workplace—whether or not they hold a diploma—are students the schools have failed.

8

What Business Can Teach Education

Accountability and responsiveness in public education cannot be legis-lated, regulated or achieved by fiat or good intentions alone. They require both incentives and disincentives. The system that best meets these objectives fairly, efficiently and rapidly is a market system.
—Committee for Economic Development,
Investing in Our Children: Business and the Public Schools

WE HAVE COLLABORATED on this book because we are convinced that a vigorous America requires vigorous schools, that a world-class America requires world-class schools. The great American experiment in self-government cannot continue without the best educated citizenry in history, and the American economic miracle—a beacon to the world—cannot continue without the finest schools human ingenuity can produce.

But fine schools for the future are not the same as fine schools for the past. We don't need more of the same, incremen-tal change. We need radical change, transforming change. By any indicator, the schools of today are not working well enough for the demands of tomorrow. High dropout rates, low test scores, alienation, and low morale are a formula for continued failure.

Public education in this country is in crisis. America's public schools graduate 700,000 functionally illiterate students every year, and 700,000 more drop out. Four out of five young adults in a recent survey couldn't summarize the main point of a newspaper article, read a bus schedule, or figure their change from a restaurant bill.

At a time when our pre-eminent role in the world economy is in jeopardy, few social problems are more urgent. Public education has put this country at a terrible competitive disadvantage.

The task before us is the restructuring of our entire public education system. We don't mean tinkering. We don't mean piecemeal changes or even well-intentioned reforms. We mean the total restructuring of our schools.

Why do business leaders care about education? They care about education for the same reason every parent in America does: education is the future. Thomas Jefferson believed that education was the *sine qua non* of democracy. Without education, democracy would falter and eventually fail. He was right.

But they also care about education for economic reasons.

No less important a thinker, Adam Smith, the great Scottish economist and a contemporary of Jefferson's, thought education was of paramount importance as well. In *The Wealth of Nations*, published two centuries ago, Smith observed that a nation's wealth is its people. Were Smith and Jefferson in conflict? No, they simply approached the same issue from different directions. Both would have agreed that understanding the vital importance of education is the hallmark of a free and prosperous people.

We are not advocating the mindless pursuit of the dollar or a conception of people as merely economic entities. The issue Smith raised and the issue we still deal with today is not money for its own sake, but a society with the resources to care for its people, to support the arts and culture, to permit reflection and contemplation.

One of the principal reasons we value freedom is the promise of abundance—food for the hungry, housing for the homeless, clothing for the naked, medical care for the ill. Material abundance is the precondition of artistic and intellectual accomplishment. Once it was the province of the select few, but today we have it within our power to extend those opportunities to whole societies. That is the task before us. That is the opportunity education affords.

Education's goal should be to nurture, develop, and encourage human intelligence. For it is human intelligence that produces wealth—not property, machines or physical plant. It is human ingenuity that counts. The source of the industrial revolution's abundant energy—coal, natural gas, oil—is a simple curiosity without human ingenuity. The magic ingredient is human imagination, enterprise, innovation. By itself, oil has no more intrinsic value than sand. Indeed, it is on sand that the high-tech world of the present is built. Not the shifting sand of metaphor and allegory, but the sand that is used to make silicon, the foundation of the integrated circuit, the backbone of the knowledge-based society.

How are human intelligence and imagination nurtured, developed, and encouraged? What are their sources, and what are their wellsprings for a people free to inquire, free to act, free to innovate?

Schools are the one social institution in which we all participate and have a stake. To use the jargon of policy analysis, they are the "policy variable" that is subject to change and manipulation. We can improve our schools by deliberate government action. We can hire better teachers, we can pay them what they deserve, we can strengthen the curriculum, improve tests and measures, expect more of students. In short, if we have the will we can improve our schools.

Most youngsters have a natural aptitude to succeed, if they have the support and concern necessary for full development. Those of us who are lucky enough to be born into caring, middle-class homes tend to take for granted the support and concern that provide the ingredients critical to long-term success. If your parents care and have the financial and intellectual resources to back up their concern, then America really is the land of opportunity. The schools can't do it all, but they can make the crucial difference. They can do so when they take seriously the idea that the customer is all-important. They must tailor their offerings to the needs of the customer, and they must believe that, in a fundamental sense, the student is always the customer.

Let us provide an example. In the for-profit sector the most important customer is not the "honor student," the customer who is always satisfied and gives repeat business. It's not the "regular student," either—the one who gives constructive criticism when the firm hasn't provided precisely the right combination of product and service. The competitor's most important customer is the dropout, the customer who doesn't renew and doesn't say why. That is the customer the corporation must understand if it is to continue growing as a corporation. The implication should be clear.

The dropout sends the school a message, and it is up to the institution to figure it out. Competition forces business to follow up on customer dropouts because they've moved to another vendor. In business, one vendor's loss is another's gain; but in education, it's the dropout who loses, because he has no other vendor to turn to. It is society's loss, as well, because without an adequate education, dropouts are liabilities—not assets. The simple truth is that we can't have a world-class economy without a world-class workforce, from senior scientists to stockroom clerks. And we cannot have world-class work force without world-class schools.

We are convinced that the postindustrial, knowledge-based economy requires a transformation in schooling, its organization, structure, and processes. The emphasis in the schools of the future must shift from an industrial metaphor, in which schools are organized like factories, to a high-tech metaphor, in which schools are organized like professional and scientific companies.

These companies are characterized by flat organization charts, little middle management, pay for performance, a high degree of collegiality, agreeable working conditions, heavy investments in R & D and continuing education and training for the staff. They have flexible hours, use performance measures rather than input measures, and exert a light hand at the administrative helm. In addition, they rely heavily on technology at all levels to increase productivity, improve communications, and reduce repetitive and boring tasks to a minimum.

As human capital–intensive organizations, they are not afraid to replace labor with capital when appropriate. Professionals in modern industry are expected to use computers and word processors, both to increase output and to decrease reliance on secretarial tasks. In the same way, teachers and administrators should have regular access to computers and electronic networks to expand their capacity to organize instruction and to share ideas electronically with their colleagues.

Indeed, if the public schools are to survive and prosper, they must take a page from the high-tech book. Xerox managed to do what almost no other American corporation has done—recapture market share from the Japanese. How they did it is worth thinking about. In the 1960s, Xerox "owned" the plain-paper copier industry, but in 10 short years, Xerox gave up half of it to Japanese competition. To recoup, Xerox had to become a new company. Virtually every facet of Xerox has been changed, from product design to marketing. Everything from development and manufacturing to the scheduling of lunch hours has been rethought and reworked.

Although Xerox explored product differentiation, the mainstay of the corporation has been copiers. To compete with the Japanese, Xerox cut in half its manufacturing costs and time to develop new products. Most important, quality problems were cut by two-thirds in two years. Xerox's customer satisfaction index, compiled from monthly reports of 50,000 customers, increased by nearly a third during that time. To do that, Xerox had to restructure—it had to invest in new ways of doing things.

Since 1980, the company has poured millions of dollars into automated manufacturing and materials handling, which has cut the cost of making a copier by half. Annual savings in manufacturing alone amount to $500 million. But as the *New York Times* said, "Even more important, Xerox has overhauled the very way it manages its own business. Nowadays, the bureaucracy, and much of the corporate staff, is gone." In place of the bureaucracy are entrepreneurial product development teams, crisis teams, and problem-solving teams.

The hallmark of the high-tech company of the present—not to mention that of the future—is the CEO as facilitator and orchestrator, not dictator. Performance is rewarded and incentives institutionalized. The metaphor of the successful high-tech company is the brass ring, not the whip. So, too, should it be in successful schools, both today and in the future. Administrators should serve teachers, not the other way around.

The emphasis in the school of the future must shift from teaching to learning, from command and control to autonomy, from blue collar labor to white collar, from employee to colleague, from boss to conductor. Those changes and others like them will produce a very different learning environment, one that reflects the realities, demands, and opportunities of the twenty-first century. Each of the six elements we have described in the preceding chapters plays a part in a comprehensive reform strategy we think is needed to revitalize American education. But a cautionary note is in order. Organizations are not ordinarily self-reviewing or self-reforming. Powerful outside forces are usually necessary if reform is to take place. The modern corporation offers a case in point. Its incentives to change—whether the change involves product lines, internal organization, customer relations, or management—are largely external. They are the product of competitive forces.

As the *New York Times* observed,

> Xerox, in a way, was a victim of its own early triumphs. The company's . . . first plain-paper copier, the 914, was one of the most successful new products in corporate history. Xerox had such a stranglehold on the copier market throughout the 1960s and early 1970s that it hardly paid attention when the International Business Machine Corporation and the Eastman Kodak Company began making high-speed copiers, the most lucrative part of the market. Nor did Xerox worry when the Japanese began to offer small, inexpensive copiers in the mid-1970s, an area Xerox ignored until recently. The Xerox of the late 1970s was a bureaucratic company in which one function battled another, and operating people constantly bickered with the corporate staff.

Left to their own devices, few managers or CEOs—in either the private or public sector—would change, because the attraction of the familiar, the tried and true is so powerful. That's true of corporations, labor unions, government bureaucracies, families, fraternal associations, churches, and schools. Social organizations are by their nature conservative and cautious. Ordinarily that is a virtue. As President John F. Kennedy said, "If it is not necessary to change, it is necessary not to change." True enough, particularly with large and complex organizations with multiple stakeholders.

But this is a watershed period, one in which change will occur because it must. In broad outline, the process by which change will occur in education will follow one of two forms. Either it will be freely chosen by educators and their constituents and allies, or the public will grasp the nettle and bring about changes they prefer, whether or not the education community supports them. It's an old story in democracies. We are convinced that if the education community freely chooses to implement the recommendations we have spelled out in this short book, public education will be revitalized. If it does not, public education will falter and may even fail.

The American public is too sophisticated and too serious about education reform to sit this one out. They believe in education, they know that it works and that it is the hope of the future. They will not hesitate to impose reform from the outside in. Forced reform frequently uses blunt instruments to accomplish its objectives. Let us offer an illustration, the Gordon writing rule in Florida.

Many educators complain about it, but whatever its shortcomings, the education establishment brought it upon itself. The brainchild of state senator Jack Gordon, a Democrat from Miami, the writing rule is a detailed and prescriptive approach to a pressing education problem, the widespread failure of students to learn to write. After public hearings and debate, Gordon drafted permissive legislation that provided for state reimbursement to school districts that elect to participate in the program. The program requires students (first only seniors; now all four high school grades) to write one 200-word theme a week. To give teachers time to read and grade the work, no school may assign more than 100 students a week to English teachers in the writing program, a reduction from 150 students a week in most schools.

It is widely known that students can learn to write only by writing. They must write regularly and faithfully. Their work must be read, graded, and returned. And no teacher, however dedicated, can do that week in and week out with 150 students. (It is not even clear that it can be done with 100 students, but better 100 than 150.) Florida schools could have done that on their own—no doubt the best already were doing something very much like that, at least for their honor or advanced placement students. But Senator Gordon felt that there was no other choice—if he did not act, the schools would not act.

Politics, of course, is the art of the possible, and education purists too often turn against it. It would be splendid if the schools themselves were so inspired that politicians like Senator Gordon would be content to leave them to their own devices. But so far, the schools have given no sign that they will reform on their own. It is easy to be cynical about the Gordon approach, but it is not easy to imagine an alternative as effective. If reforms of the kind that Gordon proposes do not work—and if the schools themselves do not propose better ones—the public will be left with only one arrow in its quiver: to quit the public schools altogether.

That is hardly a novel idea, but it is worth looking again at its implications. Indeed, it has already happened in many of our cities. In Washington, D.C., for example, the middle class, black as well as white, has fled to the suburbs and private schools. In 1987 the public high schools of the city enrolled 15,500 youngsters. Only 381 were white. And while we have limited data on enrollment by socioeconomic status (SES, in the jargon of sociology), we know that the black middle class has, by and large, bailed out.

Nationally, the black middle class is overrepresented in private schools, and for good reason. Education is important, particularly for groups entering the mainstream. To approach the issue from a slightly different perspective, look at the Preliminary Scholastic Aptitude Test scores in the District of Columbia. (PSAT is the practice test taken by juniors before they take the SAT. PSAT scores are used to determine winners of the National Merit Scholarship Program.) The cutoff score for merit finalists and semifinalists is a function of the number of test takers and the number of scholarships available. Each state and the District of Columbia receive a pro rata share of merit scholarships, and the larger the number of high scorers, the higher the cutoff score to win one. Washington, D.C., has the highest scores in the nation. The Washington, D.C., suburbs have the second highest, a commentary on the families and students who live in the district.

Each year, seventy to eighty merit scholarships are awarded in Washington. One, occasionally two, are won by public school students. The rest are won by students in private schools. Clearly, the best and the brightest have abandoned the District's public schools for private schools, and the public schools are failing those who remain.

What that suggests is that the conceptual framework developed by Albert Hirschman in his elegant book *Exit, Voice and Loyalty* has a strong empirical foundation in our nation's schools. Families will patronize the public schools—they will be loyal—so long as they think the public schools are meeting their needs. Indeed, they will remain, even if the schools are in disarray, if they believe they are being listened to in good faith—if they have a voice. But if the schools refuse to hear, and refuse to perform, families will exit.

That's why we care about schools and education. Our interests are both selfish and selfless. No company, no organization, can be better than its employees. Xerox spends about $260 million a year on employee training and IBM spends $1 billion; indeed, every employer in America, large or small, spends money on employee training, from the smallest mom and pop grocery which provides informal on-the-job training, to high-tech corporate giants with elaborate, formal education and training programs. But we can do no better than the graduates of the nation's schools. Business can train employees who are educated—those who have learned how to keep on learning. Business cannot train the uneducated.

Lest readers think that business is interested in vocational education, let us assure you that nothing could be further from the truth. Indeed, the last thing high-tech companies need is vocational education. They need employees who are broadly and deeply educated, "liberally" educated.

A liberal education not only imparts the great lessons of

history, citizenship, and science, it also teaches people to think, solve problems, and take risks. A liberal education prepares the individual to think independently, to step back from problems and the crowd, to be an entrepreneur and innovator. The virtues of a liberal education are the virtues of free enterprise in general and the high-tech, knowledge-based society in particular—flexibility, adaptability, inventiveness, even playfulness.

The fact is that capitalism is unruly and free-wheeling. Under that exterior, it is also disciplined, determined, and hard working. The real virtue of capitalism is that it is both individualistic and cooperative. In fact, the great contribution of the modern company to the modern economy is as much collaboration as competition. Companies collaborate by playing by an agreed-upon set of rules both within the company and between companies. Competitors play fair, but they also play hard. They play to win, and that requires teamwork and cooperation, as well as competition.

Business people care about education, not for reasons of philanthropy and altruism alone—although they are important—but for bottom-line hardheaded reasons. They care about education, because profits depend upon it. Without it, our society will founder, and our business will, as well.

The business community as a whole is convinced that America cannot compete without first-rate schools. The Committee for Economic Development has already released two major policy statements on education, *Investing in Our Children: Business and the Public Schools* and *Children in Need*. The California Business Roundtable spearheaded a major reform in California. The Minnesota Business Partnership did the same in Minnesota.

In addition, individual corporate leaders have taken it upon themselves to advance the cause of reform. Owen B. "Brad" Butler, former chairman of the Procter & Gamble Company, spoke out tirelessly on reform, before Congress and in countless public meetings and seminars. Similarly, H. Ross Perot has invested both time and his personal financial resources on behalf of education reform. And William S. Woodside, chairman of the Executive Committee of Primerica Corporation, has been an outspoken advocate of business support of public education.

To date, however, the business community has treated the schools with kid gloves. On the positive side, that restraint reflects the business community's deep and abiding commitment to public education. On the negative side, however, it spares the schools, permitting them to think that incremental change will be enough. It will not.

Business and education have largely failed in their efforts to improve the schools, because education has set the agenda. To be successful, the new agenda for school reform must be driven by competition and market discipline, unfamiliar ground for educators. Business will have to set the new agenda, and the objective should be clear from the outset—complete restructuring.

William E. Brock, former secretary of labor, has said that in the nineties and beyond there will be a job for everyone who wants to work and is educated. He might have added, a *good* job. For that is the reality of the future. Education is not only the key to jobs and wealth creation in an abstract sense, but it is also a source of economic vitality. It transforms old ways of thinking and doing things.

If wealth was once measured in gold, silver, and precious stones, it is now measured in what we know. And just as gold and other forms of physical capital are portable, so too is "human capital," the acquired knowledge, skills, and attitudes imparted by education. But human capital is portable in a special way. A thief, or even a competitor, could acquire your physical capital—you could literally lose it. But human capital is yours for life. You are what you know. And because of the Thirteenth Amendment—which outlaws slavery and indentured servitude—human capital cannot be collateralized or repossessed by another. It's yours and yours alone.

The name *Xerox* itself is a symbol of human capital. As one of the great high-tech success stories of the modern era, Xerox has name recognition so complete that the company must constantly remind people that *Xerox* is a noun, the proprietary name of a company identified with a specific process, *xerography*. It is not a generic term synonymous with the verb *to copy*. The name *Xerox* must be protected because the company is selling ideas, a process, a way of thinking about modern communication needs.

Although Xerox sells and leases machines, they are not the most important part of the business. What Xerox really sells is applied human intelligence, ingenuity, imagination, solutions to communications problems. Xerox sells exactly what schools are expected to produce, and that, too, is one of the reasons the company cares about education.

Education excellence is not just a local and state problem; it is undoubtedly our most serious national problem. In the first edition of this book we challenged the presidential candidates to rise above partisanship and adopt our ideas as their own. At the very least, we the public, the consumers of education, deserve to know what the candidates think about education and what they propose to do about it, and as former governor Thomas H. Kean of New Jersey has said, "We deserve it in plain and simple terms."

The facts are simple and irrefutable. We cannot have a world-class economy with dropout rates that average 25 percent. That they approach 50 percent in our cities is a national disgrace. The truism bears repeating: Tomorrow's workforce must be better educated than ever before.

We are not talking here about just the best and the brightest students—they are important, but we are most concerned about the least among us, the disadvantaged and the dispossessed, the poor and the discouraged. They are tomorrow's workers, too. A society is measured as much by how it treats its least well off as by what it accomplishes. And that is particularly important in a democracy.

From a business perspective, the education system presents an alarming picture. It is one in which too little is expected of too many, results are sacrificed to bureaucratic convenience, and professionalism—particularly teacher professionalism—is discouraged. The system is not just failing a large number of students—those who drop out or fail to make satisfactory academic progress—it is failing dedicated teachers, as well.

It is failing them because schools are organized to meet the challenges of the nineteenth—not the twenty-first—century. And until schools are reorganized to meet today's challenges, the system will continue to fail. Let us provide an illustration.

It's a baleful commentary on the nature of our schools that the best and brightest of our teachers are "canny outlaws."

They have to be canny outlaws to do their jobs well, for they are by nature intellectual entrepreneurs, innovators, system beaters, and rule benders. Good teachers are not bureaucratic paper shufflers. Good teachers do not fit into tidy bureaucracies, because the job of the good teacher is not to "process" students like so many file cards, but to educate them. It's hard work, but done well, it's gratifying work. It's gratifying because education is not the same as training. Education is a moral enterprise. It transmits values as well as skills in three dimensions: study, example, and practice.

Study is disciplined inquiry and work. It's what teachers assign and tests measure. It's not much fun, but when successful, it's always rewarding.

Example convinces students that study and learning are both worth doing and worth doing well. That's what we mean by teachers as role models, men and women of unquestioned integrity and dedication. Through example, they inspire.

And finally practice—learning by doing, by trial and error, by experiment and diligence. It's the basis for service to family, community, and state and also the foundation of scientific method.

If you wonder which teachers provide this balanced approach to education—study, example, and practice—remember your best teachers. They are the kind of employees that good businesses seek out, but that education systems tend to discourage. Original, irreverent, intellectually alert—these are characteristics of the teachers you remember from your own experience as students.

Teachers like those are not encouraged to join the ranks of the profession, nor are they encouraged to stay if they do join. Lockstep, myopic management is still the norm in American education today, just as it was in American business while the Japanese were relentlessly taking over market share after market share in industry after industry.

American business fell behind, not just because the Japanese were better, but because we were committed to ossified management structures. It wasn't just that our plant and equipment needed replacing. Our entire way of thinking needed to be replaced. Not just updated or revamped—replaced!

That's why today's successful companies bear little resemblance to the companies of ten or twenty years ago. Today's high-tech company is lean—it has stripped away middle management. It's decentralized, relying on the know-how and professionalism of workers close to the problem. It's innovative in the deployment of personnel, no longer relying on limited and limiting job classifications. It spends heavily on employee education and training. It invests heavily in research.

Successful companies have discarded the archaic, outmoded, and thoroughly discredited practices that are still in place in most of our large school districts. Those districts are organized like a factory of the late nineteenth century: top down, command-control management, a system designed to stifle creativity and independent judgment.

At a time when both creativity and independent judgment are critical, particularly on the part of building principals and teachers, giant school districts are organized like a dinosaur whose head is barely able to communicate with its tail, just as it was in large corporations. The modern company has decentralized of necessity—the old command-and-control structure no longer worked. Our competition was beating us with better products, because they were better organized, and they were organized with the modern product or service and the modern employee in mind. The modern employee must be better educated, better informed, more flexible than ever before because what we're paying for is the ability to think, to solve problems, to make informed judgments, to distinguish between right and wrong, to discern the proper action in situations that are necessarily ambiguous.

Indeed, the job descriptions for our technical and scientific employees—and our sales force, as well—sound much like the characteristics that make a good teacher: imagination, resourcefulness, energy, intelligence, mastery of a field, ability to communicate, and enthusiasm. But if we treated our workforce the way most school districts treat teachers, we'd soon be out of business. The Donahue report prepared in the mid-1980s for the AFL–CIO showed that the modern employee values independence, professional running room, and working conditions more than salary. That's true of labor as well as management.

We've found that productivity relates directly to the degree of freedom and independence we afford our employees. And that is precisely how schools must begin to think if they expect to attract and hold the best and the brightest.

In many of the nation's largest school districts, custodians run the buildings. Teachers can't get into their classrooms except during school hours. They can't even get keys to their rooms. Even if they could get into their schools, they wouldn't have any heat or lights. That's a typically depressing example of organizing for the convenience of administrators—and custodians—rather than the other way around.

Imagine a company where the most important employees could come to work only between 8 A.M. and 5 P.M., where the scientists, researchers, and salespeople worked precisely to the bureaucrat's clock. Professionals just don't work that way.

There are even more important barriers to excellence, both institutional and organizational. The central school district office—HQ—should be a service center, not a command post. A large organization cannot be "run" by a chief executive, unless its product is so uniform and the process of production and delivery so routine that the job is absolutely mindless. Large, complex, and creative organizations can be "orchestrated" or "choreographed" by a chief executive, but not "run." The CEO's most important job is not to crack the whip. It's to find good people, set goals, hold people accountable, reward performance, correct problems, and then step back. If the initial judgments are correct, the business will prosper. If they're wrong, all the micro-management in the world won't be enough.

Why bother to seek out and hire bright principals and teachers and then keep them on a short leash? They never reach their potential, which is bad for them, bad for students, and ultimately bad for the school district.

One way to think about this is to borrow a nautical metaphor popular in high-tech companies—employees are encouraged to experiment "above the waterline." That is, they should be innovative, experimental, entrepreneurial in ways that will not "sink" the company if they go wrong. Only when "below the waterline" issues arise, should employees go to their superiors. That maximizes both employee initiative and accountability, the best of both worlds.

Ideas like those are just so much talk until they are implemented and until resources are committed to their implementation. But money talks, and we have a very simple suggestion for any school district: Pay no one in the district—except the chief executive—more than you pay your highest paid building principal. Don't pay any administrator, whether associate superintendents, regional superintendents, directors of this or directors of that, more than building principals.

To educators, we say this: If you believe the building principal is the most important person in the education chain of cause and effect, as we do, then do what other professions do: Lawyers hire administrators to run their law firms for them, but pay them less than the partners earn. Doctors do the same thing. Educators should do no less.

Instead of a command post, make central administration a service center. Go ahead and allocate funds, but make the principal and staff responsible for spending them. Central administration should sell its services to the building; let the teachers and principals decide how much overhead they want. That will streamline middle management, we assure you, and it will put resources where they belong, in the school building. Hiring and firing should be done at the building level as well. When principals and teachers participate in the selection process in their own schools, you can be certain that quality and performance will improve. Experiments with teacher participation in hiring and promotion are already under way in places like Toledo, Ohio, and Rochester, New York.

We have laid out some lessons that we think the business world has to offer the schools, and we will hazard a guess that it is the rare school district that will have the nerve to examine this approach seriously and candidly.

In all fairness, we must admit that the business community was no less fearful about such ideas. Xerox didn't go through a major restructuring just for the fun of it, or because a friendly critic wrote a book. Xerox did it because Xerox had to. It was change or die.

The *New York Times* didn't pull its punches when it said:

> As recently as the mid-1970's Xerox arrogantly thought it had no serious competition. Now it is obsessed with it. The productivity, cost and quality of virtually every function and every task—from inventory levels to the number of drawings a design engineer turns out in a year—are compared with either the competition or the company that is considered best in that area.

Restructuring worked for Xerox. Xerox is probably the first company in an industry targeted by the Japanese to regain market share.

Restructuring is just as serious an issue for the public schools. The stakes are high and they are real.

Finally, we are often asked: If we really care about education—and particularly if we care about choice and competition—won't our reform ideas put the public schools at risk? They will. But the greater risk is to leave them as they are, to refuse to change them when we know change is what they need. The public schools must change if they are to survive. They are a set of institutions boldly marching backward into the nineteenth century, just when they should be leading the charge into the twenty-first century.

In the preceding pages we have described a six-point plan for American education:

1. *Choice.* Public schools should compete with one another. Students and teachers should be able to choose the schools they want to got to.

2. *Restructuring.* Schools should reorganize as magnet schools, be open year round, and be run by teachers and principals.

3. *Professionalism.* Teachers must take more control, setting their own curricula and raising standards to elevate their status to the level of other professionals.

4. *Standards.* Academic standards must be raised and children held strictly accountable to them. Just as it is the teacher's job to teach, it is the student's job to learn—no promotion without performance.

5. *Values.* We are producing a generation of young Americans that neither understands nor appreciates our democratic society. Our children should understand the great documents of American citizenship and the ethical, moral, and religious underpinnings of their creation.

6. *Federal responsibility.* The federal government's role in education is limited and should continue to be so. But within the limited role, the federal government should do more than it does, particularly in research.

For the reader's convenience, this six-point plan is summarized in the Afterword beginning on page 163. We have also provided a list of "resources," a bibliography for the interested layman.

Most of the ideas that we develop have track records; they have been tested, at least in isolation. What is new about our ideas is that we wove them together into a unified reform plan, based on our knowledge of the best practices in business and education. In this closing chapter, we want to make a case for market response, and argue that unless the schools make radical change themselves, change will be forced on them by their customers. If they refuse to change, they will go out of business. Better education options already exist. Is there some evidence for that assertion? Let us describe a school that opened only a few years ago, and let the reader be the judge.

The Beacon Day School in Oakland, California, sits on the "flats," an area of warehouses and light manufacturing in the low-rent district. As unprepossessing as a school can be, Beacon Day is in a converted warehouse. It enrolls 240 children, and with word of mouth, it is beginning to build a waiting list. What makes this school so interesting? Beacon Day is a genuine year-round school. It is not just run year round. Students actually attend year round. Not 180 days, the norm for public schools, but 240 days, the Japanese norm. Teachers are paid for 261 days, the number of days in our work calendar.

Beacon Day is an extended day school. It opens at 7:30 A.M. and closes at 6:30 P.M., reflecting the reality of the modern work schedule. Working parents who need adult supervision for their children find it at Beacon Day.

Beacon Day is not organized by grade levels and age groups, but by education attainment. Children are tested and placed in a teaching and learning setting that matches their achievement level. With a "developmental curriculum," students advance as they master the material. They can be taken out of school and returned to suit the family schedule—vacation or absence because of illness is not an academic liability. Indeed, the opportunity to travel becomes an asset to be exploited.

The whole school is voluntary—no one is required to go there. Unhappily for the public sector we are not able to report that Beacon Day is a public school in the narrow sense of that term—that is to say, it is not run by the public sector. Parents pay tuition, and it is a private school in terms of traditional nomenclature. But we would suggest that, in important ways, it is much more public than most public schools. Beacon Day is open to all, it is staffed by dedicated teachers, it is racially and socio-economically integrated, it is democratic in spirit. Morale is high.

The two founders of Beacon Day are from Buffalo, New York: Thelma Farley is a former public school teacher, and Leslie Medine, a former social worker. Nearly burned out by the limitations of the public sector, but devoted to education, they felt the only thing they could do in good conscience was open a private school. Their curriculum is not economic or cultural instrumentalism. Their programs are not day care for the modern economy. Their enterprise is grounded in solid pedagogical theory.

And Beacon Day has subjected itself to the most rigorous test a school can engage in—the market. Beacon Day parents pay twice for school: once in taxes—for schools they don't use—and once in tuition. (As James Coleman wryly observes, public schools not only are fully subsidized, they enjoy protective tariffs—private school tuitions—to further enhance their market positions.) Nevertheless, many parents of limited means are willing to make significant sacrifices to enroll their children in Beacon Day and schools like it because they value the education it offers.

As evidence of Beacon Day's success, a Beacon High School was launched in 1991.

The Beacon Day School is a harbinger of things to come. There are too many teachers who are true professionals who would like to do what Beacon Day has done, and there are too many caring parents to let the opportunity for such schools go unrealized.

There are examples in the public sector that make our point, as well. Though not as fully developed as the private sector, some public sector institutions have begun to move in the direction that we chart in this book.

The most important example in the nation is in the suburbs of the nation's capital, Prince George's County, Maryland. In the mid-1980s, few analysts and educators would have looked to Prince George's County for inspiration or guidance. Enter John Murphy, superintendent and public sector entrepreneur par excellence. As smart as he is tough, soft-spoken but savvy, Murphy did what great entrepreneurs have done throughout history—he took a massive problem and turned it into an opportunity. He was able to do so because he was aided—pushed is the better word—by circumstances that in structural terms were analogous to market discipline.

The discipline in this case was provided by the court that had ordered Prince George's County to integrate. Busing was not working, and something had to be done. That "something" was left to Murphy's fertile imagination.

His solution? Magnet schools throughout the district (the nation's tenth largest) to encourage voluntary racial integration. Prince George's County, bordering on Washington, D.C., has an extraordinary mix of people and geography. Part urban, part suburban, it still has a substantial rural character. It includes the University of Maryland, Andrews Air Force Base, and the nation's first planned community, Greenbelt, Maryland. Its population includes tenant farmers, poor blacks and whites, Air Force officers, university professors, black professionals, government bureaucrats of all levels—it is the nation in microcosm. If Murphy's reforms could work in Prince George's County, they can work anywhere.

In addition to conventional magnet schools, Murphy experimented with "workplace assignment schools," schools in which parents get first choice based on proximity to their place of work. He also introduced extended day programs for working families. In sum, he has done much of what we describe in this book. Like his counterparts in Oakland, he made the changes for academic and pedagogical reasons. He believed they were essential.

Murphy was convinced that the most serious problem facing his district and the nation was the "black-white achievement gap," the persistently lower scores earned by black students on standardized tests. He was determined to close the gap. That reading scores in Prince George's County improved dramatically during the late 1980s Murphy attributes to the program of choice that the desegregation order permitted him to implement.

Choice among Prince George's schools has meant not only voluntary racial integration but also higher morale, closer attention to academic performance, and finally, nascent market discipline. Perhaps the most dramatic aspect of Murphy's reform efforts was the conference room where the district principals regularly assembled to meet with him. Instead of children's drawings, the walls were covered with charts, one for each school. Each chart displayed the school's reading scores over time. Talk about benchmarking. The impact was truly dramatic. As evidence of Murphy's national impact, he has been hired by the Charlotte-Mecklenburg, North Carolina, schools as superintendent.

A final note should give all public school people pause. Once, our public schools were temples of civic virtue. They were sustained by a powerful myth of democratic and egalitarian hope. For many Americans, to attend public school was an article of faith, bearing witness to our democratic tradition. We submit that the myth is dying, that public schools no longer have a store of "mythic" capital to draw upon. Schools can no longer assume loyalty—they can no longer take it for granted.

That, above all, is the message public school supporters should take to heart. Satisfy your customers or lose them. To lose them in the eighties will be to lose them forever, for once the tie is broken, reconnecting it will be very difficult. We see that happening in our large cities today.

Once, America's best schools were our urban schools. Today

the typical parent, black, white, or Hispanic, views urban schools with alarm and skepticism. Few parents sent their children to them voluntarily. By and large, the children who are enrolled in them are there because of dire necessity.

If the flight of elites to suburban schools and private schools continues, the future of urban public education is bleak. There are solutions, to be sure, but they require tough choices by educators. The answer is not further compulsion, keeping children in urban schools against their will. The answer is to make urban schools—all schools—places where students want to go. That is the message of the marketplace. That is how corporations rise and fall. Those that satisfy their customers do well, those that do not, fail.

That means our six-point reform program—Choice, Restructuring, Professionalism, Standards, Values, and the Federal Role—should be attended to by educators with the utmost seriousness and concern. If they think the prescription is wrongheaded or mean-spirited, it is incumbent upon them to offer counterproposals of their own. It is incumbent upon them to offer them for *their* purposes, not ours. It is *their* institutions that are at risk, *their* jobs and *their* reputations that are on the line.

We have been critical of earlier reform proposals, because they lacked specificity, and we have been critical of educators, because they have been reluctant to take the difficult steps to radically restructure education. But we have at least put forward concrete suggestions, ideas drawn from America's best-run corporations and schools. In that spirit, we have approached our task as friendly, not hostile, critics. We are all in this together. But there is a sea change in the offing.

We are convinced that the schools are losing their captive audience, at least among the better off and more ambitious. And we are also convinced that monopolies, unless they are artifically propped up, sow the seeds of their own destruction. Peter Drucker observes that successful monopolies, those that enjoy a prolonged period of market dominance, create an umbrella which other, lower cost producers begin to flourish. Ironically, the monopoly, by virtue of its position, can charge artificially high prices, creating an artifically higher market for the more efficient provider as well. Only when the monopoly provider is protected by inappropriate legal buffers can the monopoly survive the pressure of the more efficient producer.

An example from recent Xerox history makes the point. As long as xerography was the most effective and reliable copying technology, Xerox enjoyed unparalleled market pre-eminence. But once other copiers came on line, Xerox was vulnerable—market strength turned out to be market weakness, because the lower-cost competition that had been sheltered under the Xerox umbrella was able to enter the fray.

When the Xerox 914 copier was introduced in 1959, many industry analysts thought it would either fail or become a rare exotic, used by a few companies that for one reason or another would find high-speed, plain-paper copying an asset. Few people outside of Xerox had the vision and imagination to see the future of copying as an integral part of the modern office.

Try now to imagine a modern office without high-speed, plain-paper copiers. They are an essential tool in the modern world—without them most offices would founder. Until the late seventies, Xerox's market position seemed to be unassailable. An extraordinary technology had been exploited in a remarkably inventive manner. But Xerox's success produced extraordinarily vigorous competition. When the xerographic process became essential in the modern office, other companies and other countries joined the party. In a remarkably short time, the Japanese designed and brought to market copying machines that were of high quality at competitive, or even lower, cost. Indeed, to the astonishment of Xerox, it turned out that some Japanese copiers could be brought to market for less than it cost Xerox to manufacture theirs.

There are essentially three responses available to a company in such a situation: roll over and play dead, petition the government for relief from the competition, or go back to the drawing board. Xerox went back to the drawing board. In so doing, Xerox not only redesigned its product line, it redesigned the entire company. Indeed, Xerox became a new company. Xerox rose to the occasion, not because business people are intrinsically more virtuous or smarter than educators, but because business, to keep its market, had to restructure or slip beneath the waves.

Who is the winner in the process? Certainly, Xerox is a

winner. But there is a bigger winner, the consumer. And a bigger winner yet—the American economy as a whole. Better products at lower prices are the secret of economic growth and the secret of creating wealth. It is to everyone's advantage that competition makes Xerox a better company.

With the virtue of hindsight, the picture is rosy. But it is important to remember that in the story of social, economic, and institutional change, there are no soft landings. That is particularly true in an atmosphere of isolation from market forces. Reestablishing discipline is hard, harder even than establishing it in the first place.

America's public schools are in an analogous position. Isolated from the play of market forces, they have lost the habit of responding to the needs and interests of their clients. And as they have come to ignore their clients, they have ignored the legitimate interest and needs of their workers. Teachers, who were once members of demure professional associations, have become the most fully unionized industry in the nation. School management was failing, school organization was irrational, incentives and disincentives were perverse, rewards and punishments were erratic. Teacher unionization was not an accident. It happened for a reason, and it happened against the backdrop of declining unionization in other fields. Teachers formed unions because they needed them. No one else looked out for their welfare.

Now, the time has come for teachers and students, workers and customers to join hands and recast the education enterprise. Each of the elements of the reform program we have sketched in the preceding chapters offers substantial promise to the nation's teachers. Choice, Restructuring, Professionalism, Standards, Values, and Federal Responsibility are the elements of a comprehensive reform strategy that will improve the lot of teachers, students, and society at large.

We close with a final observation. The single most important lesson the schools can learn from the business community is the lesson of competition. Schools have much to gain if they heed the lesson, everything to lose if they do not. The schools are not yet forced to compete, but if they continue to fail their charges, if reform does not catch hold, schools will be subject to a spontaneous market test. Bright flight will continue. The old patrons of the public schools will finally abandon them for private alternatives or for public schools that will respond. And the public schools that ignore the most important lesson of business—that markets and competition work—will wake up one morning with no one to teach and nothing to do.

Our collaboration has been singularly fruitful, because it has brought together two people with very different experiences and different views of the world. Until recently one of us was immersed in the world of corporate America, the other was a political scientist and a professional education watcher and analyst. As no two groups in America know less about each other than business leaders and educators, our collaboration has attempted to remedy that.

Because of our different experiences, knowledge, and approaches, we've been able to keep each other honest. And whatever this short book may lack, it is not conviction or enthusiasm. We both believe that the education of the public lies at the heart of the American experiment in self-government and the American economic miracle. We believe that the great legacy of American public education can be reclaimed. We believe that with this six-point plan it will be.

One of our objectives from the beginning was to get the attention of the 1988 presidential candidates; we hope the 1992 and subsequent candidates will attend to education reform as well. For it is a moving target; it is not a problem we can fix and forget. Education, like democracy itself, is a process that demands our unending attention. Just as today's problem demands tomorrow's solution, today's solution will become tomorrow's problem. We must reform our schools if our way of life is to continue; this isn't simply an issue for the 1990s–it's an issue for the next century as well. The schools will be slow to change; we have to remember that, not because we want to justify a slow pace, but because we must understand that we won't reform the schools overnight.

Reform, we should also remind ourselves, is painful and disorienting, particulary for those who are the object of it. That is true in restructuring for-profit corporations, and restructuring the schools will be no less difficult.

We must set realistic goals and timetables. The most obvious date on the horizon is the year 2000, a number imbued with almost mythic expectations. For our purposes, however, it's an ideal date, because today's first graders will be the high school graduates of the twenty-first century. That time frame gives us a built-in deadline that's manageable. We propose, then, that we set as a national goal a completely restructured school system by the end of the century.

We want to conclude this book with an admission and a challenge. Our six-point plan for reform and revitalization is not new in a fundamental sense. We have used it in abbreviated form in speeches around that nation, and we will use it again. In large measure it is derivative. The plan owes a great deal to the National Governors' Association, the Committee for Economic Development, the Education Commission of the States, the Carnegie Task Force on Teaching as a Profession, and the National Commission on Excellence in Education. And as the reader who is familiar with the president's proposal America 2000 will know, many of the ideas developed in this book appear there. That is as it should be. These ideas are not protected intellectual property; they are not Democratic or Republican, liberal or conservative ideas. They are ideas for all Americans, in the public domain, designed to help us strengthen our institutions and face the future with confidence.

The ideas in this book have a concrete track record. They are not the idle musings of do-gooders. What is new about them is that together they offer a unified reform proposal.

Our challenge to you is to take these proposals seriously— remember your own education and imagine how it would have been different with schools of the kind that we describe. Think of your own children or the children of friends who are in school today. What effect would these reforms have on them? Would school be more interesting, more challenging, more rewarding? Would the children of today be better able to face the demands of tomorrow if the schools we describe were in place? If your answer is yes, then join us in a national crusade for change, to break the lockstep of the past and usher in a future of revitalized public education.

EPILOGUE

The Postman
Rings and Rings

David T. Kearns

I ANNOUNCED MY EDUCATION RECOVERY PLAN in a
speech to the Detroit Economic Club in October 1987. An Associated Press story on it ran in newspapers across the country, and
days later I got a letter that started:

"I suspect that your recent comments concerning education
have prompted significant amounts of postal deliveries to your
office."

That was the understatement of the year! I was buried by an
avalanche of mail.

I was prepared for honest disagreement and debate about
the merits of my proposals. But I had no idea how many people
don't think there's a problem at all.

My mail was favorable, running five to one in support of
restructuring the schools. Businesspeople and ordinary citizens
were solid in their support. School superintendents were generally on the other side. In fact, the tone of many of their letters was
angry. Teachers were split down the middle between "It's great
someone's giving us support" and "How can you criticize us
when we're doing such a good job?"

The most disturbing letters came from educators who wrote that things are wonderful in their town, and they don't know what I was talking about. In effect—"Our kids are doing fine, so stop complaining."

The superintendent of a southern state's school board association wrote to say: "You owe an apology to every person connected with public education." His schools have one of America's highest dropout rates and he wants *me* to apologize. But what bothered me most was the superintendent of schools of a Detroit suburb who wrote to say, "None of the school districts I am familiar with fit the description I read in your comments."

Here's a man who is literally within walking distance of one of the nation's largest school districts—one that has been shaken by student homicides, sky-high dropout rates, and rampant underachievement—and he says he's not familiar with those problems.

I'm using these letters to make a point. We're not going to be able to fix the schools unless people in responsible positions understand that this is a national problem that affects every American. Educators, in particular, can't just sit back and say that because their town's schools are fine, the nation's schools don't need fixing.

As the saying goes, you have to see past your own backyard. A school board member from a New York suburb, for example, wrote to say my remarks were "offensive and dangerous," that the dropout rate in her town was only 2 percent, and that "suburban schools are doing a good job."

I'm sure they are, and frankly, she is to be congratulated for any part she had in it. But it doesn't really matter that her town has a low dropout rate when across the country, our public schools are in disarray. Nor can I share her optimism about suburban school districts. Sure, a lot of suburban students go on to college, but they spend a lot of time in remedial courses once they get there. Parking spaces, I'm afraid, are the most important issue for many of our suburban high school kids.

I just wish letters like that were the exception, but they were typical of my mail from the education establishment. One school superintendent wrote to charge that my statistics—which were drawn from solid research data—were unfounded. Others bragged about low dropout rates and their graduates going on to college.

I heard from principals, too. One got a dozen students to write that their school was doing great (it is), and that while some of my proposals sounded fairly good, they just didn't apply to them.

Another principal wrote from Wisconsin to say that his state had "the top test scores in the nation." But a letter from a Wisconsin teacher said: "I can only agree with you one hundred percent. In my district," he wrote, "the teachers have not been allowed to have any discussion or to provide any input on any issue for the past eight years. The teachers are still in the trenches trying to do their jobs, but it is getting more frustrating every year. There is no one to turn to. I can assure you that changes will not come from within. Please help. It may already be too late."

That tone of desperation permeated many letters from teachers. Superintendents and principals—when they mentioned teachers at all—talked about their low pay, but the teachers who wrote complained about lack of respect, autonomy, and professionalism.

Some teachers wrote of their efforts to buck the system. A former high school industrial arts teacher in Colorado wrote about his efforts to apply his experience as a machinist in industry to teaching his students, but they were functionally illiterate and couldn't read simple scales or transpose fractions. "Appalled at this state of affairs," he said, "I brought this up in a staff meeting and was rebuffed by the administration . . . "

They felt that kids going to vocational school didn't have to know how to apply academics. When asked how their students would eventually be able to set up and operate the coming computerized manufacturing machines and systems, the administration replied: "That is the foreman's job to show them what to do and how to do it."

No foreman will ever teach those kids to operate modern sophisticated equipment, because they won't be hired in the first place. And if they somehow do get through the door, they'll need intensive, long-term training before anyone would ever let them near today's expensive, complex machinery.

That explains why industry faces a $25 billion annual bill just to give people the basic, essential skills that make them employable. It's outrageous that school administrators won't insist that their students master the basic skills they need to get a job.

An English teacher from Long Island, New York, put his finger on a big part of the problem: "Defensiveness is rampant whenever the subject of change in structure or routine is mentioned."

I've found that too many educators take well-founded criticism of the *system* as malicious criticism of themselves. And too many admit that the system is a mess, but won't take the next step and recognize the need for radical change.

A professor of educational administration at a California college criticized my description of the school system as "a failed monopoly." Then he described the "vast, dedicated majority of public school teachers and administrators who work within unfavorable conditions, well beyond their assigned hours," forced to use outdated equipment, and without office space for meetings with parents. I wrote back that it sounded like a failed monopoly to me. It's the *system* that's failing those dedicated teachers and administrators, as well as their students.

One teacher wrote to say he didn't appreciate my comments, but then went on to complain: "We are working under adverse conditions, no money, no cooperation from school boards, an administration interested in the appearance of a building and grounds, instead of what goes on in the classroom. . . ." Other teachers wrote to tell of how they buy supplies with their own money, stay late to tutor slow learners, and buy sandwiches for hungry kids.

One letter like that really got to me. It was from a teacher in Arizona who wrote, it's "heartwrenching to pick up a paper and read time after time what a poor job our schools are doing." She went on at length about the problems classroom teachers face every day, how hard she works, and how dedicated she is. But she closed her letter—as several other teachers did—with a request for a job at Xerox.

"I wouldn't require much in the way of salary," she wrote, "as I have never made much in the way of salary anyway. A little respect, recognition, and appreciation for my contribution would be nice though." I hope she stays in teaching—she sounds like the kind of teacher we need. But she also demonstrates my point that unless we change the system, we're going to lose the good teachers we have and we'll fail to attract the talented people our schools need.

The way to change the system is to aggressively press for structural changes. Change won't come by taking the advice of one teacher, who suggests "telling them [educators] what a good job they're doing." Nor will it come from pointing the finger at other sectors of society.

Many people wrote to say that we can't blame the schools for society's problems. They correctly point out that many children come to school hungry, abused, depressed, and suffering from poverty. But we can't wait to solve all of society's problems before we improve the schools. In the past, our public schools educated multitudes of children who came from poor families, whose living conditions were appalling, and who didn't even speak English. But they did the job, and we can't expect less of them today.

In fact, the bleak lives of disadvantaged and dispossessed children is a compelling argument for making school restructuring a priority. For a lot of youngsters, the only good thing that happens to them happens at school—a teacher's smile, the feeling of accomplishment when they master a math problem, the excitement of going on a field trip.

If we can make our schools better, we'll have a better chance to help those children lead useful, productive, happier lives. Shifting the focus away from changing our schools only means deferring change, letting the problems sink deeper, defeating the hopes of the generation of students now in our classrooms. Our deep social problems cannot become an excuse for the school's failures. They should be a spur to change the system to better serve the victims of those problems.

Kenneth H. Maurer, superintendent of Metamora Township
Schools in Illinois, should have the final word on this issue. He
has one of the toughest core curriculums in the state, and in an
article he wrote for the *Peoria Journal Star*, he pointed out:

> We in education have to work in the areas we can control. We
> cannot solve the home training problem or the ethics problem
> unless we adopt the kids, marry the single parent, and take
> total control and responsibility for raising all the children.
> This is obviously not practical. . . .
>
> Educators have two choices: we can wring our hands and
> blame school failure on the things we cannot control, such as
> American ethics and lack of training in the home, or we can
> work to improve the things we can control.

Some of his peers don't understand that. One school
superintendent in Connecticut told a newspaper that our public
education system is doing better than ever—with one small exception. "We have yet to find a way to educate an economic
underclass in society who represent mostly the minorities." he
said. "We have been making improvements, but we haven't been
able to get them implemented."

That "economic underclass" he dismisses as the "exception"
happens to include the half of all minority children growing up in
poverty and dropping out of school. And he forgets that a third of
our future workforce will be minorities!

I took a lot of flak for suggesting that every student who
enters school should graduate with the core body of knowledge
needed to succeed in today's world. Some of my correspondents
insisted that you can't educate everybody—there would always
be some who couldn't make it. I find that frightening. Just whom
should we leave out? And what percentage of dropouts and
functional illiterates is acceptable? When I hear arguments like
that, I have to think they're talking about consigning somebody
else's kids to failure—not their own. Blaming the victims of our
schools' failures is an old and tired cop-out.

In his "Keeping Up," column for *Fortune* magazine, Daniel
Seligman wrote that it is "incredible" to expect every student to

master a core curriculum. He says IQ tests show that most American children are too dumb to learn, and we should adjust our public schools accordingly. IQ tests are a pretty shaky argument, and I think it's dumb to use them as an excuse to give up on our children and on our country's future. It is an outdated elitist argument, born of the nineteenth century and hardly fit for twenty-first century economics.

After World War II, the Japanese changed from an elitist to a mass education system. But they changed up, not down. In Japan today, *every* student has to meet the same high standards. The Japanese believe that what really counts is not innate talent, but hard work.

I refuse to believe that American kids are less capable than others. Our kids are under-performing because the system is under-performing. There are no unteachable children—all normal healthy children are capable of learning. A restructured school system that fosters new learning methods and makes both students and teachers accountable will educate all of our kids.

But not all the responses to my proposal led to heavyweight discussions about educational theory and practice. Some hit close to home. The first rule in a company like Xerox is don't make your customers angry, and I guess I broke it. The school systems I criticized are also Xerox customers—good ones. And some of them let their disagreements with my proposals overflow onto their business relations with our sales people.

One school superintendent wrote our district sales manager that "since Kearns is criticizing the schools, we'll just have to take a closer look at the copier competition." Fair enough, and if we can't meet the competition, we deserve to lose the business. But could he subject his schools to the same market test?

A more cheerful note was struck by a thick packet of letters I got from an elementary school class in upstate New York. Their teacher used the news reports of my speech to get the students thinking about the education debate. Then she had them write me with their own views. That's a good example of creative teaching.

I got a kick out of those letters. Some of those kids are really on the ball. One budding supply-sider wrote that he disagreed with my plan because it would raise taxes. A classmate took my proposal for state funding of pupils to mean they'd get pocket money from the state, and he liked that notion. One boy wrote that he didn't care for the idea of so many tests, and I responded that life was full of tests and he'd have to get used to them early.

But what impressed me about the kids' letters was their respect for their teacher—and their defense of teachers in general. One girl wrote, "How can you say what you did when you're not a teacher? You were just a student in a different time. So, our class wants you to come for two days to teach us. You must do everything a real teacher would do. Then you can write another article."

That wasn't the only such invitation I got. One school superintendent even offered to switch jobs. "Trade places with me for one year. I'll bet my house and lot that I will run Xerox better than you can run my school system." I turned him down, frankly admitting that I wasn't qualified to run a school system, and I sent him the full texts of my speech and my education recovery plan.

He wrote back, "I apologize. I reacted to a newspaper account of your speech and did so prematurely. I have to agree with almost everything you said in your speech and your recovery plan."

I just wish more of his colleagues shared his open-minded approach. Certainly, some of our schools are doing a good job. But we'll never be able to compete in this global economy unless they all do.

I got a letter from John Howard, the principal of Belmont High School in Los Angeles, challenging me to come and visit his school. "I'll bet you've never been in a real inner-city school before," he wrote. He was right. But by the time I could take him up on his invitation early this year, Howard had been promoted to an administrative job.

At his suggestion, I visited Los Angeles High School instead. LA High's principal, Patrick deSantis, runs a good school. The school's motto is "We Care," and it shows. They set up a press conference for me with the editor of every school newspaper in the Los Angeles City Unified School District, about fifty kids in all. Talking to those students proved what I had suspected all along—they really do care about what happens to them and to their schools.

I've been speaking out on education reform for some time now, but I believe that what happens at LA High, and at schools just like it across the country, has more bearing on our future than anything I can say from the most prestigious speaking platforms. You see and feel things inside a school that you can't see, let alone feel, looking in from the outside. The American public school classroom is this country's future in action.

Public education holds the key to America's future, and that future is at risk. We can change our system of education and compete, or we can continue to ignore the problem and take the downward path to national decline. But instead of taking strong, positive action, we're still debating whether there's a problem at all.

If this epilogue has a single purpose, it is to call attention to the debate and bring it to an end. The schools need radical restructuring immediately. Time is running out, and I am convinced that we will not get the changes we need until everybody understands that we are dealing here with no less than a national survival issue.

Parts of my six-point program have already been implemented in this country. Not widely implemented, but you can find bits and pieces of it here and there, and they all work. They have worked well enough and long enough to become living examples of school reform.

Credit the teachers who have made them work in the only place that counts—the classroom. Credit the inventive and resourceful front-line superintendents who put them in place—Fernandez of Miami, Reveille of Buffalo, McWalters of Rochester, Murphy of Prince George's County, Maryland. I am sure there are others and I am surer still that there will be many others to follow.

They are the heroes of the American education revolution. They are the heroes of this book.

AFTERWORD

The Education Recovery Plan for America in Brief—1988 Version

THE FIRST WAVE OF REFORM has broken over the nation's public schools, leaving a residue of incremental changes and an outmoded educational structure still firmly in place.

The second wave must produce strategic changes that restructure the way our schools are organized and operate. It must recreate a public school system characterized by accountability and performance.

Despite its interest in education, the business community has been disappointingly unspecific about education reform. All of us who have been critics of public education can no longer enjoy the luxury of criticism without accepting responsibility for suggesting ways to change the system. Our stake is too big.

If current economic and demographic trends continue, American business can expect to spend $25 billion a year in remedial training programs for new employees. Public education has put us at a competitive disadvantage—our workforce doesn't have the skills an information-based economy needs.

Business and education have largely failed in their efforts to improve the schools, because education set the agenda. The new

agenda for school reform will be driven by competition and market discipline, unfamiliar ground for educators.

Business will have to set the new agenda, and the objective
should be clear from the outset: a complete restructuring. Here
are six steps to education recovery.

Choice
Public schools in America have failed as protected monopolies. They should succeed in a free market governed by supply
and demand, where individual schools compete with each other
for faculty and customers.

Teachers would not be bound to a specific school. They
could market their skills to any school in their district or region,
just as if they were in the private sector.

Children could attend any public school in their district or
region—no longer would they be assigned by neighborhood.

States would fund children with comparable needs equally,
without regard to tax base or neighborhood. If a child changes
schools, state money follows him. Children with special learning
needs would get proportionally more.

Restructuring
Every public school district with 2,500 or more children
(there are 3,800) should reorganize into a year-round universal
magnet system. Schools would be free to implement new teaching strategies and learning methods. They would become special
centers of competence in such areas as science and mathematics,
telecommunications, and the performing arts.

Principals and teachers would run their schools with complete academic and administrative autonomy—the district office
would become a service center. Schools would determine their
own specialties, set their own curriculums, and compete with
each other in a new education marketplace fueled by academic
diversity and free choice. Racial balance would be maintained,
and special efforts made to inform minorities and the poor of
their options.

Schools would be open year round with a new flexible term
that would allow students to complete their education at their

own pace. The traditional grading structure would be eliminated. Students would complete the work required at one level before moving on to the next. They could advance quickly in subjects they master easily, but more slowly and deliberately in subjects that are harder for them.

States would insure minimum levels of school performance by testing students annually. School-by-school ratings and comparative studies would be available to parents. Schools that persist in poor performance would be closed.

Professionalism

A free-market public education system will require teachers trained to use diversity in education and apply it in the classroom. These teachers will set their own curriculums, select their own textbooks, and share in the direction of staff development.

Standards will have to be raised for licensing, employment, and retention. New standards should emphasize academic knowledge over methodology—what teachers know is far more important than how they are going to teach it.

Undergraduate degrees in education should be eliminated. All teachers should get a bachelor's degree in an academic subject. A fifth year of preparation stressing classroom experience under a master teacher should be required before licensing.

Teachers should create a national certification board along the lines recommended by the Carnegie Forum on Education and the Economy. The board would certify advanced levels of preparation and performance beyond state licensing.

Salaries should be based on a combination of performance and longevity, not just on longevity alone. Teachers with specialties in short supply should be paid more. Board-certified teachers should be paid more.

Standards

Academic standards must be raised, and all students held strictly accountable to them. Just as it is the teacher's job to teach, it is the student's job to learn—no promotions without performance.

Elementary schools should require foreign languages, music, geography, and history, and they should provide an introduction to classroom computer technology.

High schools should eliminate the academic distinctions that send some students to college prep courses and consign others to vocational shops. All of our children should be expected to master basic skills and core subjects that let them function easily in our society. At a minimum, high schools should require of every student the flexible term equivalent of:

- four years of English
- three years of math
- three years of history
- two years of the same foreign language
- two years of a natural or physical science
- one year of computer science

Students must maintain a C-minus average in every subject to participate in extracurricular activities.

Values

We are producing a generation of young Americans that neither understands nor appreciates our democratic society. Our schools must teach a love of democracy, and ensure that that love is passed on from generation to generation. Our children should understand the great documents of American citizenship and the ethical, moral, and religious underpinnings of their creation. Schools should not proselytize on religion and morality, but neither should they ignore their important role in American history.

Federal Responsibility

The federal government's role in education is limited, and should continue to be so. But within that limited role, the federal government should do more than it does.

Up to $50,000 in matching funds should go to school districts that agree to design a universal magnet system.

A "venture capital" fund of $40 million should be created to help finance innovative experiments in teaching and school organization. The $40 million fund amounts to $1 per student in the public school system.

College loans to student teachers should be forgiven in return for specializing in critically needed skills or for agreeing to teach in hardship areas.

Public education is a $220-billion-a-year business, but the federal government spends only $100 million on research to support it. At least three times that amount should be appropriated for research on school and classroom organization, learning theories, and instructional techniques and emerging educational technologies.

The National Assessment of Educational Progress (NAEP)—known as "the nation's report card"—is the major vehicle for nationwide data collection on school and student performance. As noted earlier its current budget request is for $28.1 million. A free-market public education system would welcome the increase. It would allow NAEP to compile state-by-state data for the first time, and would permit testing beyond reading, writing, and math to include a wider variety of subjects, such as science, geography, and history.

The federal government should fully fund Chapter 1 and Head Start, as recommended by the Committee for Economic Development in its two policy statements, *Investing in Our Children: Business and the Public Schools* and *Children in Need: Investment Strategies for the Educationally Disadvantaged*.

RESOURCES FOR REFORM AND RESTRUCTURING

The business leader, educator, or private citizen who wants to know more about education reform and renewal has numerous sources of information to turn to. Indeed, so copious has the outpouring of learned books and reports been that not even the specialist can be sure that he or she has read them all.

For readers who wish to get more involved or to become better informed, Denis Doyle offers these capsule reviews of important books, magazines, articles, and periodicals. They are designed to satisfy the discerning generalist, provoke the discriminating expert, and lay the groundwork for the interested amateur.

America 2000: An Education Strategy (Washington D.C.: U.S. Department of Education, 1991).

The education plan of the "education president," this short booklet lays out a dramatic proposal for transforming American education. In this work of Secretary of Education Lamar Alexander and his close advisers, four parallel "tracks" are spelled out. The two most important are (1) a massive private sector fundraising effort to secure $180–$200 million for a New American Schools Development Corporation, an R & D enterprise that will design the school (or schools) of the future, and (2) a proposal that the Congress appropriate $535 million for a New American School, one in each congressional district. The other two tracks link adult and continuing education (traditional Department of Labor concerns) and children's services (traditional concerns of the Department of Health and Human Services).

America's Textbook Fiasco: A Conspiracy of Good Intentions, by Harriet Tyson-Bernstein (Washington, D.C.: Council for Basic Education, 1988).

This short, eminently readable book is written by one of the nation's authorities on textbooks and textbook adoption procedures. It is published by what was heretofore a "voice in the wilderness"—an advocacy group founded more than thirty years ago, when education reform was not fashionable. The council has been unstinting in its support of a few simple ideas: all children can learn; content, not process, counts; good literature is essential to a child's intellectual and moral development; and textbooks are the single most important element of the school.

American Business and the Public School, edited by Marsha Levine and Roberta Trachtman (New York: Teachers College Press, 1988).

A Committee for Economic Development publication, this is the serious, detailed sequel to *Investing in Our Children,* the CED education policy statement. The first half of the book contains commissioned studies of major corporate involvement in education, including that of Honeywell, Metropolitan Life, Burger King, Murry Bergtraum High School for Business Careers, the Public Education Fund, and the Boston Compact, as well as a "tale of two studies": the California Business Roundtable and the Minnesota Business Partnership. The second section considers funding strategies, program participation, and the policy arena. "Must reading" for those serious about business and the schools.

Black Education: Myths and Tragedies, by Thomas Sowell (New York: David McKay Co., 1972).

America's most thoughtful and articulate black conservative, Sowell writes with passion, conviction, and knowledge about the plight—and opportunities—of American blacks. He examines the tough issues without empty moralizing and presents a view heard only infrequently in most policy discussions.

Business Means Business about Education: A Synopsis of the Business Roundtable Companies' Education Partnerships is the June 1989 sequel to *The Role of Business in Education: Blueprint for Action*, a booklet published by the Business Roundtable in 1988.

Members of the Business Roundtable believe that "while American education has made undeniable progress in recent years, the pace of this progress is not keeping up with the pace of change in business, technology, and commerce." This seventy-five-page reference source shows that the BRT members act on their beliefs. It provides capsule descriptions of the education activities of member companies from Abbott to Xerox, including contact names and phone numbers. It is an invaluable resource for anyone concerned about the role of business in education.

Business and the Schools (New York: Council for Aid to Education, 1989).

This booklet's fifty-eight pages provide a comprehensive review of the business/school relationship, why it exists, and what many corporations have done to improve it. It describes the issues that influence school reform, "what's right for your corporation," and how to develop a school program. It also provides a "sample of business/school initiatives."

Children in Need: Investment Strategies for the Educationally Disadvantaged, a statement by the Research and Policy Committee of the Committee for Economic Development (New York: Committee for Economic Development, 1987).

The second policy statement in a series by the distinguished Committee for Economic Development, this short book is as important for who says it as for what is said. The statement is the product of months of deliberation and discussion by the CEOs of major corporations (and several university presidents), who do not make recommendations about spending more tax monies lightly. It reflects the CED's continuing interest in education as an investment, rather than as expenditures out of operating budgets (an idea they first developed in the pathbreaking *Investing in Our Children*, cited later in this section).

Choice in Education: Potential and Problems, edited by William Lowe Boyd and Herbert J. Walberg (Berkeley, Calif.: McCutchan Publishing Corp., 1990).

This selection of essays on the subject of choice was commissioned by the editors, who themselves hold different views on this volatile subject. The list of authors is a "who's who" of education policy analysts, and the book belongs in the library of anyone concerned with the subject of school choice.

Choice in Schools in Six Nations, by Charles L. Glenn, with a Foreword by Lauro F. Cavazos (Washington, D.C.: U.S. Department of Education, 1989).

The author is director of desegregation for the Commonwealth of Massachusetts and has used "choice" as a successful integration strategy in that state. Currently, about 25 percent of Massachusetts children attend "choice districts," a remarkable accomplishment that has received little attention. Glenn's quiet style of management is echoed in this thoughtful and impressive study of what the international competition does. In other countries families are able to choose among schools, not just public or government run, but also public and private. Why? In most cases, to preserve religious liberty—youngsters in almost all the advanced democracies select a school with a confessional tradition (atheists are free to be "free thinkers").

Controlled Choice in Massachusetts Public Schools, by Charles L. Glenn (in *The Public Interest*, No. 103 (Spring 1991).

This recent compelling article was written by the most knowledgeable person about choice in the United States or abroad. In addition to his full-time responsibilities as director of desegregation for Massachusetts, somehow Glenn finds time to write articles and books. They are gracefully written, rich in detail and understanding. His is one of the most thoughtful minds writing about—and actually running—education programs today.

Educating America: Lessons Learned in the Nation's Corporations, by Jack E. Bowsher (New York: John Wiley & Sons, 1989).

When this guru of corporate education and training joined IBM thirty years ago, total revenues were less than $1 billion per year. When Bowsher recently retired as director of Education External Programs, the IBM education budget alone was nearly $1 billion per year—not counting the salaries of employees in training. Factoring in that cost, annual training expenditures at IBM are more than $2 billion per year. Why? Because it pays. As Bowsher demonstrates, employee education and training pay, just as research and development, market research, and good design do. Lessons for the nation's schools abound in this comprehensive book.

Education by Choice: The Case for Family Control, by John E. Coons and Stephen D. Sugarman (Berkeley: University of California Press, 1978).

Still one of the best books about education choice, it is a book written from a moral and ethical—not an instrumental— perspective, a rarity in education today. Could the ancient Greeks (for that matter could Alfred North Whitehead) really believe that we could have a national debate about education and never discuss its moral and ethical dimensions? If you find the idea horrifying as well, you'll find Coons and Sugarman refreshing reading, even though the book was published more than a decade ago.

Education for Life: A European Strategy, edited by Kari Kairamo (United Kingdom: Betterworths, 1989).

The work of the European Roundtable of Industrialists, this book is available in an excellent executive summary from the Brussels offices of this European equivalent of the American

Business Roundtable (BRT). Like the CED study in the United States, the book is as important for who wrote it as for what it contains. The European Roundtable is a fairly new organization, formed in anticipation of European economic integration, which will go into full swing in January 1992. This study looks at human capital formation. A sample recommendation: Offer a new "pan-European baccalaureate degree." To earn it, a student must, inter alia, demonstrate mastery of three European languages: his native tongue, English, and a third language.

Education Reform: Making Sense of It All, by Samuel B. Bacharach, with forewords by Governor Thomas Kean and Governor William H. Clinton (Boston: Allen and Bacon, 1990).

At 440 pages, this is the "complete guide" to education reform: where it has come from and where it appears to be going. In securing twin forewords by Governors Thomas Kean and William Clinton, Bacharach set the stage for what the book contains: a balanced set of essays covering every aspect of education reform. Contributors include Ernest Boyer, Michael Kirst, Bill Honig, Larry Cuban, Mary Hatwood Futrell, Albert Shanker, Robert Reich, Denis P. Doyle, Adam Urbansky, Arthus Wise, and Bruce Cooper.

Escalante: The Best Teacher in America, by Jay Mathews (New York: Henry Holt and Co., 1988).

This is the true story of Jaime Escalante, Bolivian immigrant and teacher extraordinaire. Mathews, *Washington Post* bureau chief in Los Angeles, followed Escalante (who was also the subject of the hit movie *Stand and Deliver*) and gives us an absorbing biography that is a pleasure to read. It also sends the very important message that we can learn from Escalante, apply his lessons, and know that high expectations get results.

Federal Aid to the Disadvantaged: What Future for Chapter 1, edited by Denis P. Doyle and Bruce S. Cooper, with a foreword by Sally B. Kilgore (Philadelphia: Falmer Press, 1988).

A compendium of commissioned papers about Chapter 1, written by the nation's leading education policy analysts, commissioned by the editors for a major U.S. Department of Education conference on the subject, the book reviews the program's history and recommends changes and improvements. Ideas for improving the program range from modest to massive. Conferees agreed that increasing flexibility is essential, including such previously radical ideas as making Chapter 1 funds available for after-school, weekend, and summer programs (rather than "pull out" programs during the day); the most radical ideas (advanced by Doyle, Cooper, and John Chubb) were to "voucherize" Chapter 1 and let the funds follow the student to the school of choice. This idea is not as unlikely today as it was when the conference was held.

The Fourth R: Work Force Readiness (Washington, D.C.: National Alliance of Business, 1988).

This "guide to business-education partnerships," is an important source of information on the subject. It describes the benefits for business in getting involved with education, the return on investment, case studies of business-education partnership development, and the types of involvement; it concludes with partnership profiles, an appendix designed to stimulate interest in what business can do.

High School: A Report on Secondary Education in America, by Ernest L. Boyer (New York: Harper and Row, 1983).

Boyer, eighth president of the Carnegie Foundation for the Advancement of Teaching, was commissioner of education in the Carter administration and is a former chancellor of the State University of New York. With the assistance of a group of researchers, he has written an imposing book about American high schools. Boyer is convinced that the high school is "the most crucial and unifying institution for strengthening education in America" and is widely read and quoted. It is a book that should be in the library of everyone interested in school reform.

Horace's Compromise, by Theodore F. Sizer (Boston: Houghton Mifflin, 1984).

Written by one of the most knowledgeable educators in the nation, this work is a powerful evocation of a dedicated teacher's life both inside and outside the classroom. The book captures the day-to-day ambience of teaching as well as the successes and failures a dedicated professional deals with. Written with verve and style, the book is already a classic. Before undertaking this writing assignment, Sizer was dean of the Harvard Graduate School of Education and headmaster of Phillips Academy at Andover. He is now chairman of the Education Department at Brown University, where he continues to write and lecture as well as oversee the Coalition of Essential Schools project.

Hunger of Memory, by Richard Rodriguez (Boston: Godine Press, 1987).

This is an autobiographical account of a Mexican-American student's education, from poor student in a parish school in Sacramento, California, to scholarship student at Stanford University and the University of California at Berkeley. This poignant work is at once a deeply personal story of one man's education and a universal commentary on education. A gifted writer, Rodriguez emphasizes that formal education draws us out of the intimacy and warmth of family, onto the stage of history—a painful but necessary odyssey from "private" to "public" life.

Illiberal Education: The Politics of Race and Sex on Campus, by Dinesh D'Souza (New York: The Free Press, 1991)

D'Souza, an Indian (from India) with Portuguese ancestors (hence the name), has produced a tour de force that is all the more remarkable for his age—under thirty—and the reaction it has produced. Praised by a wide variety of critics—Martin Halperin of the ACLU; Martin Peretz, editor-in-chief of *The New Republic;* Tom Wolfe, author of *Bonfire of the Vanities;* Robert H. Bork, unsuccessful Supreme Court nominee; Eugene Genovese, author of *Roll Jordan, Roll*—D'Souza's book is a balanced and striking critique of the modern university as it has lost its intellectual and normative anchor.

In the Name of Excellence: The Struggle to Reform the Nation's Schools, Why It's Failing, and What Should Be Done, by Thomas Toch (New York: Oxford University Press, 1990).

One of the nation's foremost education reporters, Toch has covered education for the past decade and began his current book several years ago, when the reform movement was young. He brings experience, knowledge, and an easy writing style to a subject badly in need of all three virtues.

The Japanese Education Challenge: A Commitment to Children, by Merry White (New York: Free Press, 1987).

Available in a paperback edition, it is not only the best book available about Japanese education, it is also one of the best about American education. White traces the cultural and historical roots of Japanese education, as well as the "policy" process that led to the current system and its implications for the United States. Perceptive observation, careful analysis, and a thorough-going scholarly approach combine to produce an unusually readable and thought-provoking book. White's central admonition is on target and explains why the book is so interesting and useful: "We should hold Japan up as a mirror, not as a blueprint."

The Last Little Citadel: American High Schools since 1940, by Robert Hampel (Boston: Houghton Mifflin Co., 1986)

The Last Little Citadel describes the changes that have occurred in American high schools over the past fifty years. And change they have. One little-noted fact is that the number of high schools has remained virtually constant over that period, while enrollment has increased astronomically. Why? As the population grew, high schools just got bigger, losing their sense of intimacy and moral authority.

The Myth of the Common School, by Charles L. Glenn (Amherst: University of Massachusetts Press, 1987).

A rare book by an unusual individual. Director of the Bureau of Equal Educational Opportunity, Commonwealth of Massachusetts, Glenn is also an Anglican priest, with a largely black congregation. Using impeccable research and accessible and lucid prose, Glenn raises the most important issue of all: What is the normative and moral dimension of schooling? Convinced that education is first and last about transmitting values, Glenn tells us "the story that has brought us to our present moment of conflict and confusion regarding the role of the public school in American society," as reviewer Richard John Neuhaus observes.

A Nation at Risk, by the U.S. Commission on Excellence in Education (Washington, D.C.: U.S. Department of Education, 1983).

The work of a distinguished blue-ribbon education commission established by then–U.S. secretary of education Terrel Bell, it remains the report of reports. Not only did it provide a national imprimatur of our worst fears about education decline, it also focused the nation's attention on the issue. Although critics accused the authors of hyperbole, the words still have a prescient ring: "If an unfriendly foreign power had attempted to impose in America the mediocre educational performance that exists today, we might well have viewed it as an act of war." Millions of copies were distributed by the Department of Education, and it remains a "must read" for anyone interested in education reform.

A Nation Prepared for the 21st Century: The Report of the Task Force on Teaching as a Profession, by the National Center on Education and the Economy; chairman, Lewis M. Branscomb (chief scientist, IBM).

Released in July 1986, this report made a difference. The task force's central finding was that the nation's schools were inadequate, for teachers as well as students, and its central recommendation—the establishment of a National Board for Professional Teaching Standards—has been implemented. The report gave new impetus to the movement to increase standards for entry into the profession and to "restructure" schools.

Network News & Views, compiled by the Educational Excellence Network (a project of the Vanderbilt University Institute for Public Policy Studies).

This monthly publication for network members provides copies of education and education-related articles from sources across the nation, including the major newspapers and magazines. Much more than a clipping service, it includes carefully selected articles with introductory commentary by Chester E. Finn, Jr., a network cofounder. The Vanderbilt connection notwithstanding, the not-for-profit Education Excellence Network operates out of Washington, D.C. For information call (202) 785-2985.

Phi Delta Kappan (published by Phi Delta Kappa, the education honorary society, Bloomington, Indiana).

The magazine for the serious education reader, it emphasizes "research, service, and leadership." Its scholarly articles are informative and enlivened with cartoons. The Annual Gallup Poll of the Public's Attitudes toward the Public Schools is published each September. The 1991 annual pool continues the process, making it one of the richest sources of education data available, particularly longitudinal data. Perhaps not surprisingly, although Americans tend to give the nation's schools low marks, most respondents with children in school give their own schools good marks. Notably, inner-city blacks in the Rust Belt continue to be the most critical of all groups about the quality of their children's education because they have so much riding on school quality.

Politics, Markets and American Schools, by John E. Chubb and Terry M. Moe (Washington, D.C.: Brookings Institution, 1990).

The education book of 1991, this is the blockbuster the

education establishment loves to hate. Stories about its impending publication surfaced years before its release, and the intensity of anticipation was equaled only by the intensity of the reaction when it was published. The rebuttals and critiques have flown fast and furious, which in this case means that Chubb and Moe have done something right. Publication by the Brookings Institution made the book all the more sensational—Brookings is generally viewed as liberal and Chubb and Moe's thesis is conservative. They argue that it would be a very sensible thing to let youngsters attend the schools they want to, public or private, using public funds to do so, as long as the schools meet certain minimum standards. This is the way schools are financed in all the other developed democracies (save only Sweden, which has even lower test scores than the United States).

Public Schools by Choice: Expanding Opportunities for Parents, Students, and Teachers, edited by Joe Nathan, with a foreword by Minnesota governor Rudy Perpich (St. Paul, Minn.: Institute for Learning and Teaching, 1988).

Joe Nathan, formerly a public school principal, has become, over the years, an indefatigable champion of public (not private!) school choice. An articulate spokesman for his point of view and a peripatetic traveler, Nathan is a member of the President's Education Advisory Board (where he makes no bones of the fact that, on the matter of private school choice, he disagrees with the president.) Nathan writes widely and well, and this is a good introduction to his thinking.

Results in Education: 1987, 1988, 1989, 1990, 1991, The Governors' 1991 Report on Education (published by the National Governors' Association), with a foreword by Thomas H. Kean, governor of New Jersey.

This compelling document addresses the need for education reform and what to do about it. The work of the nation's governors, it has the authority of a document prepared by people who know what the stakes are as well as who's in charge. It takes a realistic look at what must be done and provides evidence of political will and muscle to do it. As Michael N. Castle, governor of Delaware notes, "If in the past few years we have made progress toward better schools and better educated students, toward higher classroom standards, it is because we began by asking basic questions about how to make our education system more effective."

Schools across Frontiers: The Story of the International Baccalaureate and the United World Colleges, by A. D. C. Peterson, with a foreword by His Royal Highness the Prince of Wales (La Salle, Ill.: Open Court, 1987).

The International Baccalaureate is one of the most interesting and challenging reform ideas advanced in the twentieth century and deserves much more serious attention than it receives. Among other things, it is a degree recognized anyplace in the world, and it sets, and meets, very high standards—not so high they cannot be reached, but high enough to be challenging. It is not too much to assert that were there an International Baccalaureate program in most school districts in the nation, we would not be confronting a national education crisis. A highly intellectual and demanding program, the International Baccalaureate should be considered by every district in the country.

Separation of Church and Child: The Constitution and Federal Aid to Religious Schools, by Thomas Vitullo-Martin and Bruce Cooper, with a foreword by Denis P. Doyle (Indianapolis: Hudson Institute, 1987).

A comprehensive review of *Aguilar* v. *Felton,* the case that ended twenty years of U.S. compensatory education programs for children in religious schools. Although it is true that some aid is still provided, the terms and conditions are now so cumbersome and onerous that the program is a shadow of its former self. The authors are internationally recognized authorities on private education and Chapter 1 and produced a comprehensive document on the subject. The foreword argues that nothing short of a Chapter 1 voucher program will do, an idea Justice Powell's concurring (and decisive) opinion invites.

The Shopping Mall High School: Winners and Losers in the Educational Marketplace, by Arthur G. Powell, Eleanor Farrar, and David K. Cohen (Boston: Houghton Mifflin Co., 1985).

This is the first comprehensive treatment of modern American education, written by three authorities on public and private education. It traces the evolution of the "shopping mall" high school, characterized by its breadth rather than its depth. Quintessentially trendy, the shopping mall high school tries to offer something for everyone, thereby offering little to the discerning student or teacher. The study is evidence that the road to hell is paved with good intentions.

Taking Charge: State Action on School Reform in the 1980s, by Denis P. Doyle, Bruce S. Cooper, and Roberta Trachtman, with a foreword by David T. Kearns (Indianapolis, Hudson Institute, 1991).

An update of an earlier coauthored work by Doyle and Terry Hartle (*Excellence in Education: The States Take Charge*), this book provides a comprehensive review of what the states have done over the past decade as the senior partners in the education reform movement. The authors conclude that much earnest thinking and many solemn pronouncements produced precious little in the way of real reform.

Teacher (published by Editorial Projects in Education).

This monthly publication reaches 270,000 teachers. It is designed to serve teachers the way *Education Week,* its sister publication, serves administrators and policy makers. *Education Week,* a weekly tabloid, has become the nation's education newspaper of record. *Teacher* will provide the information teachers need to assume the dominant role in the education movement, leading their profession into the twenty-first century.

The Unfinished Agenda: A New Vision for Child Development and Education, a statement by the Research and Policy Committee of the Committee for Economic Development (Committee for Economic Development, 1991).

With three books on education and child welfare, the Committee for Economic Development is a serious player in the policy arena. Each of its policy statements is carefully researched, clearly written, and most important, reflects the views of some of the nation's most important CEOs and university presidents.

We Must Take Charge: Our Schools and Our Future by Chester E. Finn, Jr. (New York: Free Press, 1991).

The latest contribution to the education reform movement, *We Must Take Charge* is written by one of the most knowledgeable education writers in the nation. Finn, former assistant secretary of education for research and improvement is also former head of the National Assessment Governing Board; in addition, he founded and oversees the work of the Education Excellence Network, a resource without peer. The dust jacket includes endorsements from Secretary of Education Lamar Alexander (the endorsement predated his appointment) and from David T. Kearns (now deputy secretary of education), which sums up the book: "a provocative and challenging book by one of America's most thoughtful and responsible education writers. Finn brings high intelligence, a gift for language and high moral purpose to the undertaking—everyone concerned about the future of our schools should read it."

What Do Our 17-Year-Olds Know?, by Diane Ravitch and Chester E. Finn, Jr. (New York: Harper and Row, 1987).

Among the most knowledgeable education analysts in the country, both authors are professors of education: Ravitch at Columbia University's Teachers College and Finn (he was formerly U.S. assistant secretary of education) at Vanderbilt University. They are cofounders of the Education Excellence Network, a membership organization for education writers, analysts, teachers, and policy makers who care about excellence in education. *What Do Our 17-Year-Olds Know* is a sobering *tour d'horizon* of what our seventeen-year-olds *don't* know. More than half don't know in which century the American Civil War was fought. In the modern world, ignorance may be bliss, but it also spells economic and political danger.

What Works: Schools that Work: Educating Disadvantaged Children, with a foreword by William J. Bennett (Washington, D.C.: U.S. Department of Education, 1987).

By the mid-1970s, it had become fashionable to assert that "nothing works," a nihilistic sentiment if ever there was one. It fell to Bill Bennett, the secretary of education liberals love to hate, to produce an argument disproving the conventional wisdom that no one knew how to improve schools. In a less supercharged environment, educators might have given Bennett the approval he deserved for producing such a book, for it was a vote of confidence in both teachers and schools. Its authoritative and homespun observations were good when they were released, and they hold up. Good advice is good advice, and *What Works* is nothing if not good advice.

Workforce 2000: Work and Workers for the 21st Century, by William B. Johnston (Indianapolis: Hudson Institute, 1987).

Commissioned by then–U.S. secretary of labor William T. Brock, this popular work is the most comprehensive, compact statement of the problem available. Beyond defining the problem, Johnston proposes solutions and areas that require change and restructuring. *Workforce 2000* draws the connection between education and economic productivity in a way that even the layman understands. The book has a practicality occasioned by Johnston's experience serving in the Carter administration and a long view afforded by his time in a think tank.

About the Authors

David T. Kearns is deputy secretary of education in the U.S. Department of Education. From May 1985 until May 1991 he was chairman and chief executive officer of the Xerox Corporation in Stamford, Connecticut.

Kearns joined Xerox in July 1971 as a corporate vice-president. He was named president and chief operating officer in August 1977 and chief executive officer in May 1982. While with Xerox, Kearns was a member of the Business Roundtable, the Business Council, and the Council on Foreign Relations.

Kearns has served on the advisory board of the RJR Nabisco Foundation's "Next Century Schools" program, which has made nearly $20 million in grants to thirty schools across the nation. Kearns also has been an adviser to the American Express National Academy Foundation.

Kearns does not receive royalty income from sales of *Winning the Brain Race*. His royalties have been made available to the Institute for Contemporary Studies to advance the ideas set forth in this book. No official endorsement of this book by the Department of Education is intended or should be inferred.

Kearns was born August 11, 1930, in Rochester, N.Y., and graduated from the University of Rochester in 1952 with a degree in business administration. He and his wife, the former Shirley Cox, have six children, Katherine, Elizabeth, Anne, Susan, David T., Jr., and Andrew.

Denis P. Doyle has been a senior fellow at the Hudson Institute since 1986. For five years before that, he was director of Education Policy and Human Capital Studies at the American Enterprise Institute, and before that, a federal executive fellow at the Brookings Institution.

While at AEI, Doyle was codirector of the Committee for Economic Development's path-breaking study and policy statement, *Investing in Our Children: Business and the Public Schools.*

Doyle is currently the principal consultant to the Burger King Corporation annual "In Honor of Excellence" symposium, which honors the nation's teachers and principals of the year.

As a public speaker and lecturer Doyle has spoken on education issues in Australia, Austria, France, Germany, Great Britain, Japan, and Thailand. His government service includes an appointment as assistant director for school finance and organization at the National Institute of Education and director of the Education Voucher Demonstration Program at the U.S. Office of Economic Opportunity.

Doyle has written widely about education for both scholarly and popular audiences. His articles have appeared in *Business Week, Phi Delta Kappan,* the *Times Education Supplement, Teachers College Record,* and the *College Board Review.* His op-ed pieces appear regularly in the *Los Angeles Times,* the *Washington Post,* and the *Wall Street Journal.*

He is the coauthor of three other books on education, *Excellence in Education: The States Take Charge* (American Enterprise Institute, 1985), *Investing in Our Children: Business and the Public Schools* (Committee for Economic Development, 1985), and *Taking Charge* (Hudson Institute, 1991).

Doyle was born April 22, 1940, in Chicago, Illinois, and received his BA and MA in political theory from the University of California at Berkeley. He and his wife, the former Gloria Revilla, have two children, Alicia and Christopher.